This book is dedicated to:
Chris Searle, for his invaluable
Mrs Elisabeth Goffe, for her he
faith in me.
All the pensioners who wrote to

GW00363977

The Alienated
growing old today
by Gladys Elder OAP

Edited by Christine Bernard
Photographs by Mike Abrahams
Introduction by JB Priestley

**Writers and Readers
Publishing Cooperative**

Text copyright © the estate of Gladys
Elder 1977

Photographs copyright © Mike
Abrahams 1977

Published by Writers and Readers
Publishing Cooperative
14 Talacre Road, London NW5 3PE

Designed by Christine Morgan

Typeset by Caroline MacKechnie

Printed and bound in Great Britain
by Redwood Burn Ltd., Trowbridge
and Esher

Published with financial assistance
from the Arts Council of Great
Britain

Contents

What do you see nurses
    What do you see?
Are you thinking
    when you are looking at me
A crabbit old woman
    not very wise,
Uncertain of habit
    with far-away eyes,
Who dribbles her food
    and makes no reply,
When you say in a loud voice
    'I do wish you'd try'
Who seems not to notice
    the things that you do,
And forever is losing
    a stocking or shoe,
Who unresisting or not
    lets you do as you will
with bathing and feeding
    the long day to fill,
Is that what you're thinking,
    is that what you see?
Then open your eyes nurse,
    You're not looking at me.
I'll tell you who I am
    as I sit here so still,
As I use at your bidding
    as I eat at your will.
I'm a small child of ten
    with a father and mother,
Brothers and sisters who
    love one another,
A young girl of sixteen
    with wings on her feet,
Dreaming that soon now
    a lover she'll meet:

A bride soon at twenty,
 my heart gives a leap,
Remembering the vows
 that I promised to keep:
At twenty-five now
 I have young of my own
Who need me to build
 a secure happy home.
A young woman of thirty
 my young now grow fast,
Bound to each other
 with ties that should last:
At forty my young ones
 now grown will soon be gone,
But my man stays beside me
 to see I don't mourn:
At fifty once more
 babies play round my knee,
Again we know children
 my loved one and me.
Dark days are upon me,
 my husband is dead,
I look at the future
 I shudder with dread,
For my young are all busy
 rearing young of their own,
And I think of the years
 and the love I have known.
I'm an old woman now
 and nature is cruel,
'Tis her jest to make
 old age look like a fool.
The body it crumbles,
 grace and vigour depart,
There now is a stone
 Where once I had a heart:
But inside this old carcase
 a young girl still dwells,

And now and again
　　my battered heart swells,
I remember the joys,
　　I remember the pain,
And I'm loving and living
　　life over again,
I think of the years
　　all too few — gone too fast,
And accept the stark fact
　　that nothing can last.
So open your eyes nurses,
　　Open and see,
Not a crabbit old woman,
　　look closer — see ME.

*'Kate', the writer of this poem, was unable to speak, but
was occasionally seen to write. After her death, her
locker was emptied and this poem was found.
(From* Elders, *Reality Press, ed. Chris Searle.)*

I am deeply sorry that Gladys Elder, after years of bad
health, died before I had a chance of reading this book
of hers. It would have given me enormous pleasure to
have congratulated her on it.

In the endless campaign waged by the old against
poverty, neglect, insensitive administration, this book
is a report from the battlefield. Even in her very title,
The Alienated , she shows her understanding of
the central problem of old people today. The point is
that during the last twenty years or so we have largely
stopped seeing our old people simply as Grannie or
Grandpa, but almost as members of a strange species,
not at all ourselves simply further along in life. They are
much more part of a problem or a series of problems,
rather than people who happen to have lived a bit longer
than the rest of the population.

At 82 I write as one of the old myself, and certainly
know some of its pains and penalties. On the other
hand, I happen to be fortunate in my circumstances. To
make a simple point — I feel the cold much more than I
used to do, but luckily I can turn on the heat.

Two things have struck me particularly in Gladys
Elder's account of old age. They are the continuing
desolation and growing terror of cold damp rooms, and
with them the increasing loneliness of so many old
people. This loneliness is far worse than it used to be,
when families tended to live in settled communities, for
in these days they tend to break up and go away, and
often lose touch with their aged parents. As one widow
reports here, 'I am only 62 but I feel 100. My children
have left me and seem not to care whether I am alive or
dead. They are both married . . . I cannot bear Sundays,
so on Saturday night I take some very strong
tranquillisers, which keep me dazed all day Sunday . . . '
No doubt more efficient medical care has kept people
alive, who at an earlier time would have died. But it is

no use keeping people alive unless they are fully alive, and as we learn from this book, if we do not already know it, a host of old people are probably ready to welcome death because all the warmth and sparkle, fun and affection, have vanished from their lives.

Quite rightly we are spared no disturbing facts in this book, for it is not intended to be pleasant light reading, and is indeed a brave, vigorous protest against wrong attitudes, inadequate pensions and a good deal of stupid administration. I hope it will be widely read and taken to heart.

J B Priestley

Gladys Elder

It was during my recovery from a bout of severe
depression a couple of years ago, that a doctor said to
me: 'Why not write a book about old age?' The
suggestion caught fire for I knew already that something
was very wrong with our society — old age should not
be the way it is for the majority of our elderly. So, like
an aging Christopher Columbus, I set out on my voyages
of discovery. I began to talk to all the elderly around me.
I tried to cultivate insight, understanding and patience,
and as I pondered on the life stories I pieced together I
became angry. I watched my acquaintances shopping. I
had no difficulty in seeing the economic limitations, the
scraping and stinting to which so many are condemned.
Sometimes I sat at home, reflecting, thinking back over
the years, seeing those lives against a familiar back-
ground — my own. I thought of the devastating times
my elderly neighbours had lived through, of their
deprivations so stoically borne — and my anger
increased. Anger is a fine spur and very soon I had
gathered together enough material to start along the
hard road of authorship. For, growing with this anger,
I had a vision. A vision of comfort, peace and rest for
the elderly, achieved not by charity and well-meant aid
from the outside, but by the concerted actions within
this group, in other words, *by themselves*. My book is
an attempt to point the way — for, my friends, there is
indeed a way, several ways, of achieving this vision. As
economic troubles continue to bear especially heavily
on us, the many problems we have to face — economic,
social and psychological — increase daily. As do our
numbers. The population in Great Britain has increased
greatly during this century and today there are more
than 7,000,000 people over the age of 65. But while
the number of those aged between 15 and 60 has merely
doubled between 1900 and 1971, the number of over-
sixties has almost quadrupled in the same period. At 75,

I know very well what aging is, what it feels like after a lifetime's struggle, to find oneself among society's cast-offs, duly labelled and slotted into the compartment called OAP. Having suffered the various problems as they exist today, I hope to pinpoint the areas where decisive action can and must be taken.

In primitive societies a corner by the fire was the most the elderly could hope for. Yet even now, in spite of the vast increase in material comfort that is widely available, this 'corner by the fire' is still out of reach for many of today's shivering elderly. Successive governments have ensured that pensioners are given a standard of living that just supports them, teetering on the edges of the subsistence level. But they are not the only enemy; for reasons we shall later examine, the *expectations* of many old people are deplorably low: independence and self-esteem have traditionally been equated with earning capacity. Conversely, state money has been equated with loss of self-respect and feelings of worthlessness. Because of this conditioning, concerted action has been slow and many thousands of people continue, in stoical silence, to subsist rather than live. For British pensioners are without economic power and thus, in a consumer society like ours, without any power at all.

Books on old age by sociologists, psychologists and gerontologists are growing in number, a hopeful sign that the subject is at last receiving due attention. *Yet none has been written by an OAP*; the distinction makes me feel I am well-placed to plead this case. I have been lucky in finding a new identity at the Open University where I am following a degree course. Here I am recognised as a person — that is, as a student, not merely as an OAP. The interest and publicity that has followed this recognition has given me the strength to fight.

It could be said that the plight of the elderly has already been put too frequently. But I firmly believe that only constant repetition of the facts *as they are* can bring about the urgently needed changes that will improve our lives — and indeed the lives of the future elderly, today's middle-aged, probably now at the peak of their careers, yet, living as they do in our inflated economy, with little or no savings. The confidence I have gained through my new status has given rise to a resolution to fight whole-heartedly for the following:

1 A general recognition that the old are alienated by our society and the acceptance of the elderly as *people* — little can be achieved until this important fact has been assimilated.
2 Representation in *all* unions at committee level.
3 New research into the maintenance of health and mobility in old age.
4 Realistic pensions that bear a direct (and instant) relationship to the cost of living.

In the next chapters I shall examine the various courses needed to put these four ideals into practice. But first we must see how and why the rot, a legacy from an older society, sets in . . .

Gladys Elder, 1975

Chapter 1
Metamorphosis

*'Mr M is nearly 80. His ground floor flat is in bad
condition. He is very confused, does not know who
the landlord is. Council gave notice to quit, verbally,
because he is blind. One week's notice only. Woman
friend helped him and kept him company. Council
refused permission for them to live together so they
married before moving into a housing estate. She died
soon afterwards. Mr M is now very lonely. Volunteers
visited him at Christmas. Council complain his rent is
in arrears. It was later discovered this was because he
couldn't go out to pay it . . . '*
(From a Task Force report.)

Franz Kafka's novel *Metamorphosis* is, I think, the most
terrifying tale ever written. It begins: 'As Gregor Samsa
awoke one morning from uneasy dreams, he found
himself transformed in his bed into a gigantic insect'.
His family's reaction is first one of revulsion, then
kindness, finally contempt, merging into total neglect;
not only had he become a revolting object — he could
no longer fulfil his function as breadwinner for the
family.

The parallel is clear in society's treatment of the aged.
It refuses them the necessary minimum, thus
condemning them to extreme poverty, to slums — such
as in the case quoted above — ill-health, loneliness and
despair, asserting that they have neither the same needs,
nor the same rights as others in the community. In
Britain today when the cost of living is still spiralling
rapidly, the pension increases offered to the aged almost
immediately become farcical, the cost of living having
already risen beyond the level of each new increase.
Those who have won rate and rent rebates are more than
likely to have these rebates decreased, thus all but
cancelling out whatever advantage might have been

gained by the original pension increase.

Simone de Beauvoir, the French author, asks 'Are the old really human beings?'[1] They are treated as outcasts, she says, and not considered 'real people' — apparently they have neither 'the same needs or the same feelings as others'. She points out that there is an enormous difference between the wealthy and successful elderly, and those of us from the working class who have retired, often living on inadequate pensions, trying vainly to catch up with the soaring cost of living. 'The class struggle,' she writes, 'governs the manner in which old age takes hold of a man: there is a great gulf between . . . the wretchedly pensioned ex-worker and an Onassis.'

People are poverty-stricken (says John Galbraith) *when their income, even if adequate for survival, falls radically behind that of the community. They cannot have what the community regards as the minimum of decency, thus they cannot wholly escape the judgement of the larger consumer that they are indecent. They are degraded for, in the literal sense, they live outside the grades . . . which the community regards as acceptable.*[2]

In another context, Dr Alex Comfort writes;

Poverty is a great robber of self-esteem; failing health and and the infirmities of old age in no way boost the morale, nor does society's attitude help to sustain a sense of identity. And once the mirror-image, so laboriously fashioned throughout a lifetime, is shattered, how many are able to acquire a fresh identity? This is especially difficult when self-evaluation has always had to battle against society's attitudes towards those given a low status in the social hierarchy.[3]

Wearing, like the Star of David worn by the Jews in

---

[1] See page 140 for text notes throughout.

Hitler's Germany, the label OAP, the mass of pensioners are treated as children, lumped together regardless of their right to as much dignity and respect as any retired professional man or woman. Would anyone, for instance, dare to apply the designation 'OAP' to a retired judge living on a state pension? It has a wholly working class connotation, with overtones suggesting that OAP's are the recipients of philanthropy — the Welfare State grandiosely distributing alms to the maimed and old. For pensioners have taken the place of the indigent poor of the past: while groups like 'Help the Aged' appeal for funds and thus salve a thousand consciences. As for the powerful media, the advertising industry has long since divided the nation into six social categories; the very bottom one (labelled E) covers state widows, pensioners, casual or low-grade workers — a position not unlike the untouchables of India. And how does a pensioner on a low income manage to exist? Why, like those indigent poor of the past, by hunting round for centres where cheap lunches are served (soup kitchens); buying secondhand clothing from jumble sales; by having to struggle, with the help of the more fortunate members of the community, for special benefits and reduced transport fares: in short, by pleading need, showing their sores and sacrificing their pride.

I was first amused and then angered to read Dr Joan Gomez, who has this to say about the aged in her *Dictionary of Symptoms* [4] : 'Unfilled leisure-time is psychologically dangerous; it causes teenagers to make nuisances of themselves, and older people to make miseries of themselves.' The same source supplies this example of patronising disparagement:

Make friends, but do not hanker after those in full flurry of activity . . . If you are past seventy, the middle-aged may have minds too agile for you. Your own contemporaries tend to self-centredness, though they are worth cultivating. You will find the greatest expanse of common ground with children.

In just such a manner have minorities everywhere been .
stigmatised as being mentally inferior at one time or
another. Suddenly, come seventy — metamorphosis!
Does it perhaps depend on class and status? The average
age of politicians, members of the judiciary and religious
hierarchies is, after all, pretty high — imagine the
reaction of some of our high court judges if they were
seriously told to run off and play with the children!

Dr Thomas Arei, a consultant psychiatrist writing in
Age Concern says that:

*Old age in our society is held not only in low regard but
in contempt. But despite this, we still maintain the myth
of its dignity and wisdom . . . For instance, the cardinal
status of the elderly as the repositories of wisdom and
respect is not available to them even though we make a
pretence that it still is.*

If the world in old age is shrunk to the size of that of
the child, it is often because society has diminished the
old, denied them the importance of self-expression and
economic and social autonomy.

In *Our Future Selves*,[5] Nesta Roberts writes:
'Standardising old people as types is wrong; no one
expects any other age group, say the middle-aged, to be
all alike; . . . the external stigmata of old age must not
be allowed to obscure the lasting divergencies of
character.'

Realisation of our individuality (she writes) *is
particularly imperilled by the fact that, in our age,
the new Greeks are the Americans, who share the
Hellenic worship of the youthful body, while showing
no great tendency to share the Hellenic veneration for
the sage . . . It is not the easiest climate in the world
in which to be old.*

21

As the American septuagenarian columnist, Lou Cottin, puts it:

When the boss says 'you're old' — retire — get out of the way. The young must take over. 'You're old,' say our children, gently. 'Observe your boundaries. Here are the corners where you may sit quietly.'[6]

There is, he says, a subtle difference between prejudice based on age and the more easily recognised prejudice based on class, religion or colour. This discrimination has been recognised in America and termed *agism*.

I cannot sufficiently labour this point of loneliness, isolation and those painful emotions deeply suffered by Gregor Samsa, Kafka's 'beetle'. With its concomitant, depression, it is a potential killer. However, many people clutch at the remnants of their self-esteem, dependent on their mirror-image, so that they rarely admit their feeling of neglect. The following appeared in *The Pensioners' Voice:*

*Why do we have a generation of elderly people who are
growing into lonely people? An apparent reason seems
to be that families are scattered. Every day some
lonely person is asking for some contact
— some communication . . . What a tragedy . . . that
loneliness in old age is now the apparent curse of our
present society . . . We must crusade for better
communication, the younger folk must remember their
parents, and constantly we must all be good neighbours!* [7]

In 1974 *Age Concern* set up discussion groups and
handed out questionnaires to the participants. The
elderly were asked which they considered the two
major problems among the evils of old age. 82% felt
loneliness to be the worst, the other difficulties coming
way below this appalling fact. 43% said too little
money; 33% named poor health; 26% complained of
lack of help and 13% gave bad housing as their main
source of worry.

Undoubtedly, many families are themselves victims
of stress in their endeavours to meet high mortgage
rates, while carrying the additional struggle to give their
own families a better start in life. Because the
personality changes that often accompany the aging
process are not understood, elderly parents and their
families may become antagonistic, whilst the inclusion
of a parent in a small house can disrupt a family. Mores
are changing, but society still has the corpse of the
immediate past strapped to its back. One result of the
Welfare State often appears to be an abdication of
responsibility for society's casualties, though it is often
called 'respect for privacy', particularly in large cities
where neighbours are unwilling to intrude. Elderly
people, living alone, are especially vulnerable; they need
to know that those around them care for them. Family
doctors have no time these days to make regular calls,

to ensure that an elderly patient *has* recovered from an illness; they have to be called in, and many elderly cannot afford telephones — some cannot even use them.

Here I admit are two conflicting points of view, for whilst I shudder involuntarily at the thought of being at the receiving end of voluntary help, I do yet believe that a society in which all co-operate and work for the welfare of all its members is preferable to 'the nuclear family' ethos, where each unit considers the well-being only of its immediate members. But while we are a long way from either ideal, the gradual dying of the old working-class 'togetherness' is slowly proceeding. This is evidenced by the cases that come to light of helpless aged people lying alone, dead or dying, for long periods before they are discovered.

In such pockets where the working-class ethos of 'togetherness' still exists, where children marry and live near their parents and visit them regularly, it is some consolation to know that the grandmother — and even the great-grandmother — still has a useful role and is thus not so isolated. But I would conjecture that removal of young families to housing estates away from the original home may mean that soon, unless a conscious effort is made, interaction between children and grandparents will be less common. Furthermore, because of high rents and mortgages, much overtime is worked, while wives work too to supplement the income, thus leaving families with little leisure time to spend together. The demand for creches and nursery schools reflects the tendency to break away from the traditional grandmother as a proxy mother, and there has been a sharp growth in the number of registered child-minders.

Increased emotionality is often a concomitant of the aging process, even when economic conditions and status are favourable — and depression is endemic among the elderly. Is this to be wondered at when, added to physical, psychological and economic difficulties, there is a high incidence of paralysing loneliness such as was experienced by Gregor Samsa in his metamorphosis: the lonely men, the lonely widows and the lonely single women, victims of the First World War when so many young men were killed, stigmatised as being 'left on the shelf', perhaps after caring for aged parents.

Investigation into suicide confirms the claim that aging and loneliness combined are potential killers. In America the aged account for an inordinately high proportion of overall suicides. Among white males the rate was found to be *six times* greater among old people than in other groups. Characteristics of those US citizens who commit suicide in old age are: lack of employment (morale among the elderly has been found to relate very closely to occupational status), and loneliness. It also occurs among those elderly who live in the deteriorating centres of US cities where the perennial problems of isolation in old age are greatly multiplied by physical isolation in a city.[8]

In this country, Doctors Adelstein and Nardon found, in a study covering the period 1961 to 1974, that the number of suicides increased with age and was higher for men than for women of the same age (which again perhaps relates to whether or not they continue to work after retirement). This study proved conclusively that suicide among those aged 65 and over is four times higher than the 15-24 year-old age group among women and three times higher in males.

Among sufferers of chronic disease, and including psychiatric patients, evidence shows that chronic illness predisposes the sufferer to commit suicide. Together the physically and mentally chronic sick show excessively high accident rates, many of which may well be intended suicide cases. The sociologist, Erwin Stengel, writes:

Social isolation . . . is the common denominator of a

number of factors correlated with high suicide rates . . .
The highest incidence of suicide in urban communities
has been attributed to . . . social isolation
and the anonymity of life in big cities . . . As a
rule the suicide rates are proportional to the size of the
city . . . [9]

A striking discrepancy between the suicide rates of two
individual cities in the North of England was investigated
by Stengel and Cook. Paradoxically, the smaller of the
two, which had only one fifth of the population of the
other, had over a considerable period a suicide rate far in
excess of the national average and several times that of
the bigger city.

A comparative study of the relevant factors revealed that
a large number of young people had emigrated from the
smaller city owing to the decline of the local industry.
As a result, the older groups were grossly over-
represented in the population, with a consequent
increase of the death rate in general, and the suicide rate
in particular.

Apparently a similar position was noted in West Berlin.
Stengel states emphatically: 'Contrary to the popular
belief, which associates suicide with frustrated love and
"poor moral fibre", the majority of people who kill
themselves are elderly, and many of them are physically
sick.' Living alone after a life-time spent as a member of
a family can be intolerable, especially to the retired
worker suffering loss of status and companionship as
well as a serious drop in income.

Among the comfortable middle-class, one is sometimes
astonished by the lack of understanding shown of the
conditions of a large proportion of the inhabitants of
this country before and after the First World War. Yet
the history books still contain very little social history
about our recent past and we still have to turn to the
novelists for the truth. Are the historians so objective

that they cannot see humanity for history? So blinded by gazing at generalities that they miss the particular? What is wrong with our teaching that we have mature, highly-educated adults asking about the elderly poor, 'Why didn't they save for their old age?' — a question thrown at me time and time again. In many cases it has been left to the novelists to describe the realities of poverty. Walter Greenwood's *Love on the Dole* [10] is not only a novel but a social documentary; while Jack Ashley poignantly describes poverty as it existed in his boyhood in *Journey into Silence*. [11]

Kafka's Gregor Samsa carried on his back a rotting apple that had been thrown at him and become embedded in a painful, festering sore. Many of the elderly carry their own painful, festering wounds, psychological as well as physical; not only the psychological disorders that can be part of the aging process, but also the rotten apple thrown at them by society. In addition, there is the dread of crippling disablement, of becoming housebound or of accepting institutionalisation as an alternative to becoming a burden on relatives already overburdened with the stress so often experienced in contemporary society by all but the more fortunate financially.

Pious utterances, reminiscent of the attitude of the Samsa family, are poor substitutes for adequate means and recognition of the elderly as people, still the same individuals they always were, though now in need of a few extra candles on the birthday cake.

Undoubtedly the metamorphosis that does occur in appearance is as lacerating to women (conditioned as my generation has been to believing that our identity lies in our appearance) as was Gregor Samsa's changed appearance to him. The high value placed on youthful attractiveness today is evidenced by the desperate face-lifting operations which the rich often seek and in the many advertisements for cosmetics purporting to delay the effects of such ravages. 'Enjoy your age — don't

look it' runs one advertisement. My aged friends are
fortunate if they can afford a lipstick from Woolworth's.
The wrinkled skin, the sagging chin, the sunken eyes,
the thinning hair, the liver-coloured blotches on the
backs of hands, do not exactly inspire confidence and
self-respect in our society. After all, the structure and
functions of the body provide the basis for our personal
identity, yet living at social security level leaves little
margin for personal adornment or for dressing
attractively to boost sagging morale! Shopping at
jumble sales means a limited choice. In any case, in a
consumer society no effort is made to cater for the
needs of the elderly. Unable to be consumers, they
become non-persons.

Kafka wrote,

*Man only counts as a function. Society has reached the
stage where a man who has no function to perform may*

be regarded as not real, as nothing . . . swallowed up in his profession . . . turned away from the feelings of human beings.

I came upon these words recently, under the heading *It's a Crime to Grow Old*:

When you are a young man, and can work for yourself and the rest of the community, you are a KING; nothing is too good for you, for you are the producer of the wealth of the land; and so it should be. You are a member of a Trades' Union . . . and you can dictate, and, of course, it is only right that you should be considered.

This is OK as long as you last — but — we all grow old, and as soon as this comes about, you are an outcast. If you are treated unfairly (and you are, you know) you have no help from your Trades' Union — you no longer have a Trades' Union.

So, because you are old, the powers that be presume that you no longer have wants. For you are useless to the the economy of the country . . . [12]

We belong to a generation that has had the traumatic experience of two world wars, the depression of the twenties and thirties with its iniquitous Means Test, the Dole with its pejorative connotation, the 'too old at forty' syndrome. For the pensioner, the Means Test still operates in all but name, a wolf in sheep's clothing. Let your income be just fifty pence above the Social Security ceiling, and all appeals for aid meet with bureaucratic refusal, bluntly given. At all turns the pensioner is diminished. Bitterness is the inevitable result.

In 1974, after I had made a broadcast (I was writing this book at the time) I received scores of letters. This one is typical of many of them:

May I wish you luck in writing your book on the older generation. It's about time someone stood up for us. Thousands of old people . . . gave their all and risked

29

*their lives in two world wars for their king and country
and now don't even get respect but are treated like
muck . . . the people of Britain have a lot to thank most
of the older people for, but they can't get them
underground quickly enough. We know that we are not
wanted, that is why we get bitter and go back into our
shell and want nothing to do with anyone. Who can
blame us? It makes my blood boil when I see the way
old people are treated. There are too many living in
damp, tumbledown houses . . . with insufficient food or
fire . . . I am nearly seventy myself and I am looking
forward to reading your book, so best wishes and good
luck.*

In a society placing a high value on monetary returns
for services, pride and independence have to be
sacrificed if one has to accept charity. We have not *all*
grown up in the Welfare State; old moral standards have
to be painfully abandoned and in a world in which
complex changes are rapidly taking place, the aged are
soon out of joint with the times. They are in the
position of Alice in *Alice in Wonderland*: ' " . . . Faster,
faster, faster," cried the Red Queen. "I can't go any
faster," gasped Alice, whose feet had by now completely
left the ground.' One must have lived through the
period to understand the environmental and
conditioning factors that have formed the elderly of
the generation that grew up before the First World War.
They are sensitive to becoming the incubus they fear
they may be to others. The middle-aged may see in us
what awaits them and, ostrich-like, exclude us from
their clubs. This happened to a friend of mine recently,
when applying for membership in a women's social
club, where she was gently informed that 'they'
invariably preferred the over-45's to join clubs 'more
suited to their tastes'. The writer Keith Waterhouse
responds in lively fashion to this kind of thinking: 'I
wonder,' he writes, 'if old people ever get fed up of being

30

talked about as if they were completely ga-ga?' He goes on to say in the same *Daily Mirror* article, 1973:

It is one thing to be properly concerned about their welfare . . . quite another to treat them as a pack of infants. Because they have earned their pensions, it doesn't follow that they have to be patronised, or that they particularly relish a pat on the head from their juniors. This sickly and condescending approach continues down the line. 'Old people must be kept at a constant temperature,' says a well-meaning notice outside my Town Hall . . . do we have to make them sound like pet rabbits . . . ?

On the whole, it is youth today who are most sympathetic towards the elderly, less likely to regard them as society's rejects. They have their own immense problems, sources of never-ending debate, but at least they have vigour and a stake in life. They clamour for

attention and have the energy to make themselves heard. However, in its enthusiastic devotion to the demands of youth, high in spending power, society fails to listen to the weaker voices of the elderly. It is strange how people seem to think that *they* are unlikely ever to be plagued with stiffening joints or that senility could ever befuddle their senses — or infirmity make them dependent on others; or that poverty may catch up with the apparently most secure, living as we do in an unstable society. Thus, they significantly fail to recognise that values and attitudes are not immutable, but are likely to change at different stages of life and under varying circumstances; so that when their turn comes, they may not be so eager to enter a Home, nor accept alienation resignedly. Since mankind has always steadfastly refused to consider his own latter end, re-education in this sensitive area seems our only hope for future generations. Perhaps we could start by constant repetition of the old adage: It's later than you think!

How disheartening it is to read some of the pronouncements of eminent psychologists who so often get lost in generalisations. I believe there are two factors that affect efforts at objectivity: the uniqueness of the individual, and the effect of different life styles, environment and the conditioning of the researcher, who may well be class-bound, generation-bound and intellectually-bound. W. Rae Ashby has written: 'Vivid though consciousness may be to its possessor, there is yet no method known by which he can demonstrate his experience to others.'[13] Even the most perspicacious of students of human nature may fail to decipher the clues accurately. We can never do the right thing, nor make ourselves acceptable: too active, and we are labelled dissatisfied, discontented; too resigned, we are accused of disengagement.

Our problems will go unsolved, as Lou Cottin says, so long as we do not face the hate and violence to which other minorities were and are subjected. 'Our opponents mask their antagonism behind sweet words and kindly gestures — but they serve with half measures. What they give with the right hand, they take back with the left.'[14]

As another American sociologist, Michael Harrington, has written:

There is a familiar America. It is celebrated in speeches and advertised on television and in the magazines. It has the highest standard of living the world has ever known . . . there exists another America. In it dwell somewhere between 40,000,000 and 50,000,000 citizens of this land . . . They constitute 25% of the total population . . . largely comprise the aged, the unskilled worker . . . the Negro and other ethnic minorities.[15]

I find there is an under-lying feeling of loneliness in the aged, of being left behind, of having been cheated (especially in this country where hopes of a 'land fit for heroes to live in' was one of the first broken promises by political parties after the First World War). There is a feeling of bitterness, of helplessness, and in many cases an incredible stoicism displayed in face of economic difficulties and physical disabilities; a valiant attempt to retain some dignity, in many cases by an *appearance* of not caring. Then, too, the old are resigned in the face of a defeat they cannot possibly hope to reverse. For their very circumstances make them helpless, as do frustration, the discomforts and disabilities of the aging process, the economic shackles and the indignities to which they are subjected. However, underneath there is not all the resignation that some research workers imagine; slowly, but surely, a militancy, a rejection of their present position is growing among the elderly.

But before we examine this new militancy and explore ways of encouraging it, let us take a further look at the conditions of the elderly, and also see if we can discover, by examining the recent past, some of the main causes of our alienation.

Chapter 2
How it is

An old woman, her person filthy, hair lousy, clothing in rags, obviously not changed for an exceedingly long time, is found slumped in a broken armchair, in front of an empty grate, on a bitterly cold New Year's day. There is neither fuel nor food in the house. The walls of her flat are covered in dirt and hung with cobwebs. One room only had been used, a dark, evil-smelling place. A broken mattress lies on a bed thick with dust, with neither blankets nor sheets. The electric wiring is dangerous, the water is not working, the sink is stopped up. Sour-smelling milk bottles stand in a cobweb-hung kitchen. There is no carpet on the floor, which is thick with coal dust. There is neither fuel nor means of heating. After eighty years of life, her total possessions are two bars of chocolate, a pinafore, a pair of shoes, her rent book, an insurance policy and a little money in an old tobacco tin. [16]

I am not so naive as to suppose that there will never be inequalities. My concern is that while thousands of pensioners live out their lives at subsistence level, the gross disparity that still exists between the haves and the have-nots can only weaken the will to improve matters. Too many people — particularly among the elderly — feel that our system 'was and ever will be so'. I recently saw an advertisement for a private pension scheme which prophesied that in twenty-five years' time, secretaries would be earning £17,000 and chauffeurs £15,000. Thus, when the former's weekly rate is £326, I can only too easily visualise some meek pensioner of the day saying gratefully, as he collects his £32, 'I remember when the pension was only £11.60 a week! How fortunate I am — today I'm getting nearly three times as much!'

This attitude is typical of those at the end of the

pecking order, those low-paid workers who humbly accept their lot — and who can sometimes be heard berating the rebel. For, of course, a mere glance at a comparison between the position of the more affluent members of our society and the disadvantaged reveals a stunning disparity. As you lick your Green Shield stamps, ponder on these extracts from *Labour Research*, a monthly magazine of the left, which regularly prints extracts from various sources that illuminate this vividly:

Sir Richard Dobson has a great worry at the moment: what to do with the £80,000 cash payment he receives from British American Tobacco when he leaves to become Chairman of British Leyland. 'What does one do with that amount of money?' is Sir Richard's woeful cry. He doesn't need to buy a car — British Leyland will provide that; he suffers from seasickness, so he can't buy a boat; he doesn't want another house. Apart from his golden handshake he will still be receiving a nice little salary from British Leyland — £22,000 a year.
(*Daily Mail* 1.3.76)

Eighty-year-old Linda Bassett also had a worry — how to pay her electricity bill. She would only switch on her heaters when neighbours came to call. Her fear of a big electricity bill made her a victim of hypothermia; she died from cold.
(*Daily Mirror* 4.2.76)

'In these austere times, we are all having to cut back,' says heir to the Marks and Spencer fortune, Jonathan Sieff. So Mr Sieff has had to sell his 5-bedroom flat in Eaton Square, Belgravia — for 'considerably more' than the £150,000 asking price. He is moving into a more 'modest' place in Cadogan Lane, Belgravia.
(*Daily Express* 16.2.76)

A 71-year-old pensioner dying of leukaemia and lung cancer was discharged from hospital, although he was

*homeless and had nowhere to go. Eventually, he broke
a window and walked into a police station and asked to
be arrested in order to get a bed and medical treatment.
Four months later he died in the hospital wing of
Pentonville Prison.*
(*Daily Mail* 4.7.75)

*Mr Nigel Broackes, chairman of property company
Trafalgar House Investments, has at last managed to sell
his Berkshire home, Wargrave Manor. The Manor was
put up for sale at the end of 1974 for £800,000. Mr
Broackes has however now sold it at the 'giveaway'
price of £600,000 to a Swiss company. Luckily, Mr
Broackes has another home to move into; the more
modest Deanery, at Sonning-on-Thames, which cost a
mere £120,000 (before restoration and modernisation).*
(*Daily Telegraph* 18.9.75)

Governments, anxious either to score over the
opposition, or to find a whipping-boy for the country's
financial condition, are apt to lay the blame within the
ranks of the recipients of social security and the
beneficiaries of social services. Alas, some pensioners
themselves cast suspicious eyes on one another, or
castigate their own hierarchy — the workers — for
having the courage to demand a higher standard of
living. Similarly, among those earners frenetically
clinging to rungs on the social ladder, every effort to
improve the life-style of the retired worker is viewed
with grudging resentment.

Most pensioners recognise that when the social
security officer calls he is more likely to be on the
watch for any small improvements in their income,
rather than for those tell-tale signs that the allowance is
too small. Indeed, pensioners admit that they actually
appear guilty by the way they excuse themselves, feeling
compelled to underline their gratitude and minimise
their needs. This feeling of being suspected and of being
watched is a further indignity suffered by those on

Supplementary Benefit. A case was published recently where residents in a Hackney block of flats became suspicious of a man who sat in his car outside the flats for long periods over several days. After a week, someone asked him what he wanted. The driver then started up the car, dragging the questioner along for several yards. The police were called, but the man refused to state his business. It finally transpired that he was a special investigator for the Department of Social Security. He had been asked to check up on a woman suspected of illegal cohabitation while drawing supplementary benefit.

The desire of the elderly to be of service, and their craving for social contact are often exploited. One London Borough Council ran a sheltered workshop where pensioners packed thousands of contraceptives for a derisory hourly rate. I talked to a voluntary worker who had visited one such workshop, and she confirmed my fears of exploitation when she told me that she had seen a forewoman stop an old lady from talking. If she had allowed them to chat, she explained, others would follow suit instead of getting on with their work. But human beings are social animals, gregarious by nature; most of today's pensioners come from large families and are quite unaccustomed to solitary living. Relatives can be alienated by differing interests and expectations, and not least by distance itself. Suicide figures prove that the old, the sick and the lonely are most at risk. Among them too will be found the shy, those fearing rejection, people who suffer from the I-never-speak-to-my-neighbours syndrome, and others who are ashamed of their poverty and who carry it about with them, hidden, as if it were an unpleasant disease.

Let us face it: except for a fortunate minority, old age *is* intolerable, it *is* an invincible, inexorable enemy. Face this, and we have taken the first step towards making it more tolerable. While death is inevitable and

sometimes blessed, it is the slow decay that can destroy us before the final extinction. Simone de Beauvoir has listed the many famous and highly respected public figures who dreaded this period of life.[17] Churchill fought against it, although it finally destroyed him. We all know how the poet, W B Yeats, when he was only fifty-seven, but blind in one eye and threatened with deafness, dreaded old age, and his cry of protest is still poignant today —

This caricature
Decrepit age that has been tied to me
As to a dog's tail.

(I too have little sight in one eye, and know how he felt.) Nearly everyone tries to fight off the advance guard: look at the long history of rejuvenating cosmetics, plastic surgery, and the hopeful drinking of elixirs. I have yet to meet anyone exclaiming, 'Oh, I'd

love to be eighty!' The very least that society ought to
be doing is to help to sustain the morale of the aged —
indeed, I regard a consideration of everyone's self-
esteem as a fundamental social duty. Yet societal
attitudes still deny the aged such rights and so increase
the despair widely felt among the lonely aged.

A belief in the species, which is an integral part of the
will to survive and therefore a belief in life, presupposes
an acceptance of the doctrine that all individuals count
and have a right to a full life, and to the leisure that
increasing technological developments will provide. The
majority of people do feel this at heart, for it is a strange
fact that — themselves threatened with over-population
— the highly industrialised nations continue to rush to
the aid of regions devastated by natural catastrophes.

This dichotomy in our impulses, this divided self,
is only supportable because conformism makes us
accept shibboleths that hide reality, though it intrudes

sometimes, even if we only sense it intuitively.

The sociologist Phillip O'Connor has written:

The mature, self-respecting citizen is the partially divided man; he has a sense of reality, and by 'reality' he here means the poor contemporary circumstances that he has been forced to accept and that he has actually failed to understand, because the understanding of this reality provokes the vision of a better one, and thus becomes the need and the desire to change the lesser one. It is the lack of a sense of reality that produces conformism and the lack of vision which builds the pillars of society based upon it. [18]

There is another factor at work within the divided self. Erin Pizzey, of 'battered wives' fame, says, 'There is a primitive mechanism in all of us that makes us feel that misery is infectious. Those who fall foul of the broad path of success, therefore, must be kept away, lest the bad luck transfer itself to the onlooker!' This highly relevant observation is expanded on by Dr White, a psychiatrist at Tindal General Hospital, in an article discussing the social psychology of psychogeriatric problems: [19]

. . . it relieves the anxiety of people living in the same locality to have those problems – especially self-threatening ones like age and madness – removed from their midst. When there is trouble, they (doctors) . . . convince themselves of their duty to impose a solution regardless of the patients' will – indeed, the refusal of help is often held to be, ipso facto, *a proof of mental illness and hence grounds for compulsory admission to hospital under the Mental Health Act.*

Yet, he says, change may overtake us in our own later life:

. . . our desirable residences may be the faded glories of tomorrow . . . we will almost certainly find a younger

generation — for which we have neither sympathy nor understanding — tut-tutting over our way of life. And if the solutions they impose on us are not to our liking this will be a well-deserved Nemesis, for we are now setting patterns of care for many years to come.

So what are the facts that so many of our citizens shut their eyes to? I believe that only a Henry Mayhew could do justice to the many cases that have come to my notice since I started looking. I have either seen them with my own eyes, or they have been vividly described to me by friends.

In Liverpool an old woman, dying of cancer, was sent home from hospital to a cold and dirty bedroom, to a handicapped husband who drank and was deep in debt, and who had tried to kill himself five times.

An old woman in Haleswood was found choked to death from trying to eat cardboard.

An elderly man lay dead for four months in a tiny terrace house. He was found because an Electricity Board official called at the house.

Des Wilson, lately of *Shelter,* has brought the attention of the public to a number of such cases: the elderly Portsmouth woman who had been dead in front of her television set for over two months before being found; another man dead for three weeks before anyone discovered him. It was reported that four different men had died this lonely death in one block of flats in one year. An 81-year-old woman died in her home of exposure and frostbite, weighing only five stone at her death; an 80-year-old Cornwall woman lived on cat food for months before she died.

In December 1973, two cases of suicide by drowning were reported in the Runcorn press in one month alone. One was a woman of sixty, the other a retired railwayman in his seventies. He was found in the frozen canal with just his head sticking out of the ice. He left a note saying that he found it depressing when you get old and have to live on your own. He suffered from bronchitis and had confided to his two sons — who lived in the same town — that he couldn't stand the loneliness and sickness since his wife died in 1968.

And here are some extracts from a few of the many hundreds of letters I received after an article of mine appeared in the *Daily Mirror,* and after my broadcast:

'I am now 78, my wife 74 and more than semi-invalid. We are still in our damp bedsitter. We have a total income of £16.40 per week (this was 1974) and pay rent out of that. Our gas costs us between £3 and £4 per week for heating and cooking, and our laundry about 60p.'

'Our income leaves us £7.20 for food and clothing for

*two people, one of whom has to have a special diet. With
regard to the gas fire, we burn only five out of nine
burners. We really have nothing left for recreation or
clothing. This is not life; it is Hell on earth, and
thousands of my generation are living like this in
Britain today.'*

*'I am an OAP, on the outside looking in on life, in this
world of so-called affluence. We are back on the Means
Test as it was in 1918. It's a pity we were born too
soon. But I'm afraid there isn't anything we can do
about it. Some of us are very near the breadline, as it
was called in the 1918 war. The social security almost
want to know why you were born . . . We have to walk
half a mile up a big hill to get our Social Security.'*

*'I am nearly 75 and am secretary of an old people's
club. I served seventeen years on my local Council and
was Mayor in 1960-61. I want to congratulate you on
your stand and to say that you have courage and
integrity. Yes, we are last in the queue and will remain
there until we have a government that will recognise the
needs of old age, that will admit we helped to build up
the wealth of this country.'*

*' . . . Many old people have worked hard all their lives,
brought up sons to fight and die for their country, and
now they still have to suffer in their old age . . . I will
be retired very soon and would fight with you . . . It is
pitiful to see old people degraded . . . Some look lost in
the wilderness and feel outcasts. They have suffered
enough poverty in their lives — pawn shops, poor goods,
not able to afford luxuries . . . They have paid their
contribution and should get a decent living pension to
exist like human beings.'*

*'I brought up two children alone. My husband died
when I was 45, my children respectively 4 and 8. I
have had several operations and can no longer go out
cleaning, and I'm only 63 but I feel a hundred. My*

47

*children have left me and seem not to care if I am alive
or dead. They are both married . . . I can't bear Sundays
so on Saturday night I take some very strong
tranquillisers which keep me dazed all day Sunday. I
take mild tranquillisers every night during the week,
otherwise I couldn't sleep for vague pains all over. I
think it may be protein deficiency as I cannot digest
cheese or eggs. I have literally begged my son for help
. . . I have always tried to be a loving person but now I
feel like a hurt animal and am retreating into myself . . .
away from the cold heartless average person. They are
all right, have husband/wife, car, fridge, etc. They can
go on holiday. I haven't had a holiday away from my
four walls for 16 years. On the few occasions I have
seen my son . . . he has come out with some very cruel
statements. He says that surely age should have
mellowed me instead of being bitter and "This is a
material world. It's every man for himself" . . . My one
prayer is that I don't live to be really old.'*

*'I am a widow (69) and all my married life my husband
and I worked hard (we were farmers) and brought up
six splendid children, two of whom went to the war.
During the war we worked like slaves to produce good
food for the country, so misnamed 'Great Britain'.
When my husband died last year I practically lost the
sight on one eye owing to a broken blood vessel. I asked
Social Security if I was entitled to a bigger pension than
£7.10 and was told by another faceless wonder, 'Sorry,
no, you are not classed as disabled.' How inhuman I
wonder can the world become? I was able to buy a
caravan after a long search and I work to keep sane.
There are times when I want to say "Stop the world, I
want to get off." '*

*'I, too, am a rebel, but I am afraid you are fighting a
losing battle with the establishment . . . Good luck to
your book, but, believe me, I don't think it will alter
the present state of conditions one bit. I am 70, my wife*

*65, living on our State Pension and Supplementary
Benefit. I am half crippled with arthritis and also have
diabetes. At the last pension rise, my wife's pension was
increased by 43p, from £3.57 to £4.00, my pension
and social security was reduced from £10.00 to £9.90,
giving us a net gain of 23p. This I am afraid happens
every time we get an increase in pensions . . . What
really makes me see red is the way people in authority
use the excuse of the suffering of old people when
there is a strike of gasworkers, electricity or mine-
workers.'*

Task Force alone have uncovered thousands of similar
cases (more about them later on). The following
descriptions are taken from their files — some being as
recent as 1976:

*Mr F. Over 80.
Tenant of Grosvenor Estate for years. Unfurnished
cottage. During winter of 1971 Grosvenor asked Task
Force to decorate. Found green slime on stairs, water
dripping into the kitchen; living room unusable with
paper hanging down in shreds from damp. Gutter
broken and brickwork crumbled away on roof. Task
Force agreed to decorate when repairs completed.
Despite repeated attempts to get something done,
repairs not done, and Mr F. moved to another room. He
had pleurisy the winter before last, and pneumonia last
Christmas.*

*Miss C. 90's.
Agrophobic Italian lady. Written permission to have
lodgers. Mews cottage in bad state while rest of row
very smart. No electricity — gas lights. One cold water
tap outside; outside WC leaks. Has paid for own repairs.
Heart condition since last visit of landlord. Extract from
letter we received from her:*
    *'Thank you very much indeed for coming to see me.
I appreciate your kindness very much, but after you left*

*I panicked and realised I would have to face up to ——
in the event of your applying to them on my account, so
please I beg you don't go near them about me. I am too
terrified of them. They pushed me around in 1967, and
I have not forgotten that awful time they gave me . . .
You see, I have high blood pressure and heart trouble
which Dr Winkler of Tachbrook Street will confirm, and
for which I have tablets (9 a day), so you see I need
peace and quiet so please don't report anything to ——
about me beyond paying the rent. I want nothing to
do with them . . .'*

*Mrs B lives in an old people's home. She is deaf and
blind but mentally very alert. She speaks very well but
to communicate with her you have to spell words out
on the palm of her hand. She is one of the very few non-
senile residents and has complained that she is
completely isolated and that the staff do not bother
to talk to her. We have two very good volunteers visiting
her who can both finger spell very rapidly. Both these
volunteers contacted us recently as they felt that Mrs B.
was being ill-treated. They noticed that she hadn't
been washed or bathed properly. One of them was there
when she had her supper once – a plain cracker biscuit
and a cup of tea which was just put down in front of her
without any acknowledgement. Mrs B. hasn't an
independent social worker. I should like to mention
that after we took this up with the social worker . . . it
has been noticed that Mrs B. is now being bathed
properly and having her bedsheets changed regularly
(this wasn't happening before); she has also been given
a new housecoat.*

*Mrs B. brought her gas bill into Task Force during the
winter because she was unable to pay it. We wrote to
the DHSS asking for a grant towards it. Two and a half
months later (with not a word from the DHSS) the Gas
Company wrote to Mrs B. saying she was to be
disconnected in two days. She did not come into Task*

Lunch club

Force to inform us about this but borrowed the money and paid the bill. She cannot now claim having paid the bill, and she is in the position of having to repay the borrowed money to her friend.

Are we all, always, going to shrug our shoulders and say, 'Awful, isn't it, but that's just how it is!' Decent self-respecting citizens that we are, are we really prepared to let so much despair, so much misery, so much degradation, continue unabated, in the pious hope that 'someone else' will clear the mess away?

Or are we all going to think about some of the reasons why these conditions should still exist, in Great Britain, in the latter half of the twentieth century? Until the causes both of these conditions and our seeming inability to alleviate them can be found, no fundamental changes will occur. Many more old people will live and die alone, in solitary neglect, before the tide turns. But I passionately believe that some of the causes lie in the past, have never been recognised by more than a handful of thinking, concerned people, and because they underlie our social structure, make all of us uncomfortable. In my next chapter I will try to examine some of those causes which still echo and re-echo throughout our 'affluent' society. For it is not only the poor who are ever with us — it is the past as well.

Chapter 3
Finding the Present in the Past

*My family were always on the move; each street got
meaner; each house smaller. My father was a cripple, my
mother in poor health — the ultimate dread was the
Workhouse . . . The Toby jug on the dresser was always
full of pawntickets that were never redeemed.
Sometimes a man would call and another piece of
furniture would depart. Moving day for our few sticks
was fraught with suspense . . . every winter I developed
a racking cough. During a bitter winter my father
collapsed with cold and hunger and was finally admitted
to hospital with starvation . . .*
Extract from a letter written to Gladys Elder by
Mrs. Smith of Essex

We two kept house, the past and I.
Thomas Hardy

Cicero once said, not to know what took place before
you were born is to remain forever a child. How much
of the social history of the late nineteenth century and
the early part of this century is effectively taught in
schools? And how much is actually understood of what
life was like for the ordinary men and women then? To
understand the old, it is essential to have some
awareness of the social, economic and educational
factors that have moulded them. For we are all victims
of our past, shackled to it like Dickens' ghost of Jacob
Marley, trailing his cash boxes behind him for all
eternity. The 'mind-forge'd manacles' of the past
shackle many of us who have been the victims of
insecurity, of mis-education, of poverty, of the lack of
encouragement to seek the development of that open-
mindedness which might have helped us to adjust to the
so-different present. The miracle is that so many of us
have to a certain extent adapted ourselves to changing

mores and accepted, perhaps with a shrug of the shoulders, a complete reversal of traditional ethical standards.

If you want to help us integrate ourselves into contemporary society it is necessary to know something about our past; for if we must try to know and understand *you,* then you must learn to know and understand *us.* Furthermore, we have something to give, for we are the authentic links with the immediate past, soon to be lost, excepting in the books of a few writers. Even photographs do not tell you how we felt.

I think it was Toynbee who once said that people as a whole receive an education which makes them the victims of their environment, rather than of their fate. Many of my elderly friends are such victims; worse, they are victims of a past that, ethically and socially, seems to have little relationship to the present.

Most of my generation have been subjected to the rigidly fixed pattern of behaviour, traditional in the culture of the old Coronation Streets; many social changes have occurred so quickly that values have become debased coinage. It is difficult for the old to find a foothold, particularly since their meagre education and life-style — their programming — has not encouraged the development of an open mind.

80% of those retiring in 1970 (and for 10—15 years to come) had left elementary school at 11 or 14, and had not been near any kind of education or training since then . . . These people are the most disadvantaged, and are therefore in greatest need of help in negotiating the transfer from a work-orientated existence to the total leisure of retirement. The considerable incidence of ill-health and death in the first two years of retirement is perhaps due to neglected symptoms in the last years at work, and to the loss of stimuli, loneliness and a sense of uselessness. [20]

Today, for these elderly, the certainties of a lifetime

are shattered. At the same time, the great web of
kinship is fast being destroyed as work-mobility
increases and the village — or Coronation — street is
being replaced by high risers or new housing estates. In
a strange and rootless world, adjustment is very hard.
Even when we do accept the present, the present is not
static from one year to another as it used to be. Changes
occur almost from one month to another, so that there
is never a time when the old can step into the present,
as it were — for lo! as they do so, the present has
become the past. It is only too easy to feel that nothing
can be done but give up the struggle and sink into the
comfort of memories. The new generation, busy and
impatient as ever, find it hard to understand this and
can easily cause the old to become first isolated and
finally alienated.

'Each age,' wrote historian Arthur Marwick, 'must
re-interpret its own past.' Nevertheless, those alive at
the beginning of the century provide a valuable
primary source of what it was like to belong to a
certain social class at that period, even if the truth is
sometimes glamorised in an endeavour to decorate an
anecdote. In what may sometimes seem to be the
monotonous, repetitive narrative of an old man or
woman, a picture will surely emerge of their life and
of what it was like.

There are a few who have managed to throw off the
shackles of the past. The miracle is that they should be
so mentally alert when, for the first time, they are able
to resurrect what have probably been old desires and
ambitions. For the industrialism of the nineteenth
century fostered a harsh, crude life-style; and education
— such as it was — was a legacy the Edwardians
inherited. It had a stunting effect on the potential
intellectual and reasoning powers of many of my
generation, born in a social milieu where the only
available education turned them out like sausages, to
feed the industrial maw. Looking back on my own

education, I'm certain that government schools did nothing to encourage the growth of a spirit of independence.

In Scotland, where I was reared, one important prerequisite for a teacher was the ability to wield the 'tawse' (a leather strap with fingers) unceasingly, without undue fatigue. Its use, to me, was a terrifying sight, for neither of my parents ever hit me. I have never recovered from the shock of these constant lashings doled out in the classroom — though teachers did not dare to beat me or my brothers and sisters, for my mother was a dragon when roused. Indeed, I was so terrified that my mother finally took me away from school until I was seven, for it gave me screaming fits during the night. But in any case I hated school and feared it — and certainly learned very little there. Frightened of the other children, I felt it was a sort of purgatory that had to be endured for so many hours of the day.

I received all of my reading education at home and could read Ivanhoe by the time I was seven (though, knowing nothing of rape, I was puzzled by Rebecca, the Jew's daughter, whose attitude to overtures of friendship seemed to me unduly fussy). Back at school, after those blissful two years, I continued to hate it. I only once dared to ask a question. Thereafter, realising that there was nothing in the curriculum that was relevant to me, I deliberately withdrew from active participation and emerged comparatively unscathed at the age of fourteen, my only accomplishments being the knowledge of some Scottish myths (labelled 'history'), a command of the multiplication tables, and the ability to spell and punctuate (though, as I write, I realise that these are becoming rarer gifts in an age of liberal education!).

At school we were given indoctrination of the most virulent imperialistic patriotism — this, in Scotland, being combined with nationalism. On Empire Day, we children paraded with small Union Jacks singing lustily, 'Rule Britannia, Britannia rules the waves . . .', for we lived in 'an Empire on which the sun never set'. I can remember attending a small country infants' school when I was five, where we marched round singing, 'Happy little soldiers we/Marching round so steadily/ Who would not a soldier be/Hip-hip-hip-Hurrah!'

Yet, when enslaved by the poverty of the Depression, did the unemployed draw much comfort from the euphoria of Empire Day, the pride in a great and glorious Empire, the refusal to be enslaved? Did they remember this when the Means Test Officer called and they discovered that the Englishman's home was no longer his castle? Unemployment, which never dropped below 10%, reached roughly one million in the 1920's, one and a half million in 1930 — and shot up to around 23% in 1932; so that, including dependents, around *seven million* people in this country were living on the dole. (This was the period when the Means Test Officer searched the larder to ensure that no foodstuffs were available.)

This Chapter started with an extract from some autobiographical notes sent to me by a Mrs. Smith from Essex. They give excellent descriptions of life among the poor at the beginning of this century so I am quoting further extracts from these recollections here:

People can often look back and reflect on happy childhood memories. I have few that I treasure, grim stark poverty being the ogre of my past, against which my parents had to contend — and it was always a bitter, losing fight. I was born at the beginning of the century, the 'good old days' — days that were good for the lucky few, a grim endurance test for the less fortunate and the weak. I didn't have much of a start. Fed from a long tube bottle (an Edwardian monstrosity) I was soon in the Great Ormond Street Hospital with rickets . . . It's a marvel that I'm still alive to tell the tale. We were always on the move. My mother used to say, 'Don't have an elaborate home when you marry, because you'll lose it.' Men used to hammer on our door late at night for accumulations of unpaid rent, and receiving no answer nailed a 'notice to quit' order on the door. Hence our frequent departures. In an agony of suspense and fear, I would wonder whether the moving men would turn up sober (pubs were open all day and there was much heavy drinking). Meanwhile, my mother used to watch at a window in case a landlord turned up and demanded money we hadn't got.

I suffered an inferiority complex at school, having to wear adult clothing and footwear. I had a racking cough every winter, but no medical treatment or vitamins or school milk in those days. Doctor's bills had to be avoided. My mother's remedy was mustard on a flannel on my chest which produced an angry rash and was torture to endure. The alternative was Russian tallow on brown paper — but the smell was frightful.

Twice each Sunday I had a long walk to church — my mother insisted I went. It was High Church and a long service about the 'Spiritual Grace of God' etc. that I couldn't understand, and the incense made my empty tummy feel squeamish. Besides, once outside, I knew the better dressed children would make unkind remarks concerning my ill-fitting garments.

During a bitter winter, my father collapsed with cold and hunger in Billingsgate Market, and was finally admitted to hospital with an ulcerated leg and starvation. The ambulance came at midnight (horse-driven), with jingling harness, like a sleigh ride. Whipps Cross Hospital nursed him and fed him, but my mother and I had to rely on kind neighbours and 5/- a week from Masonic funds temporarily. Each week we trekked to the big house — side door please *— for the charity hand-out.*

Once my father opened a grocer's shop in a poor part of Stratford. Alas, this was an ill-fated venture. Angle

Lane, Stratford was a poor locality. Everything was sold in minute quantities, and debts accumulated on the slate. The only ones that derived benefit were the rats, mice and cockroaches. We were situated between a bake-house and a slaughter-house, and there were no 'rodent operators' in 1909. So the vermin thrived, but we didn't.

Then the 1914 war 'to end all wars' — so they proclaimed. My father got a job — it was a miracle — as a packer in a city warehouse. My mother diligently machined gas-mask cases. Our kitchen smelt like a rubber factory, but it brought in a few shillings for a brief time until my mother collapsed and died from intense cold through queuing for food, and I was alone at 14.

An illustration of the real poverty before 1914 is the following incident. Our meagre shopping was done late at night when meat was sold at cut prices — no 'fridge

Winifred Smith (Evening Echo)

then. We used to get scrap bacon at a well-known grocery store. Sawdust was scattered profusely on the floor in those days. Scrap bacon was often quite good pieces. True it had sometimes been dropped in the sawdust and sometimes had 'gentiles' clinging, but cleaned up, it was eatable. (Needs must when the devil drives.) One 3d. bundle of delectable pieces had a golden sovereign in its midst! A veritable God-send! We really lived for a week.

As teenagers we used to stroll round London during lunch time. Near Old Bailey was the warehouse of a famous perfume manufacturer (Grossmith's). We used to love to stand over the grating on the pavement and inhale the exotic Eastern perfumes. There was also an eatinghouse for working girls, situated near Cripplegate Church. A religious body of ladies served cheap meals. Bare tables, knives and forks in a large jam jar. Help yourself. The daily chant at the counter: Yorkshire

Beaufort House School — washing infants clothing 1909 (G.L.C)

Beans and potatoes, until potatoes became scarce. Bowl of pea soup 3d. You could take it upstairs or downstairs to the accompaniment of hymns on an harmonium. The suet pudding was cooked in long metal tubes and shot out at 3d. a slice, plus jam and custard. All good clean fun. All you needed was a keen sense of humour and an appetite.

Well, the boys looked smart in khaki and polished buttons. Alas, the ill-fitting demob. suits didn't glamorise the heroes. Some were unfortunate in their selection. That novel, 'Love on the Dole' isn't exaggerated.

My husband was a hard worker given the opportunity, but the jobs never lasted. Whole streets of men were idle. Speeches and protests were of no avail, promises by M.P.'s and statesmen remained just promises. It was Wigan Pier in reality.

I remember gangers who wouldn't look at a man wearing a collar and tie, and my husband adopted a 'choker' scarf. He got a job and got torn and bleeding hands working with pick and shovel for there were no mechanical devices. He even got a bike at a shilling a week and rode miles looking for work.

With the dreaded Means Test in the 1920's officials would call to see if you had anything you could sell. Sons and daughters left home because they were expected to support their parents. Then there were the Jarrow Marches and their leaders. Relief tickets created problems. Some shops didn't like them; they preferred cash customers. With coal tickets we were told if merchants had any coal left over we could have it, but cash customers first.

Christmas 1925 I had to go to the local church hall for relief tickets. My husband had gone after a half promised job. The hall was situated among the big houses often with glittering Christmas trees standing in the hall. My son was only a toddler. 'Shall we see Father Christmas?' He was excited. But the Christmas spirit *didn't extend to us. 'Where is your husband? He should come himself,' growled the man, and thumped a few shillings and a food ticket on the table. No, the Means Test of the past holds no pleasant memories for me . . .*

I myself remember the huge queues at the Labour Exchanges, the hunger marchers, the sad-faced men in their cloth caps and mufflers; the pathetic bands playing in the streets of London, begging for money, composed of men who had hiked there in the hope of obtaining employment; the idle mills, the smashed machinery; the men, who, after lengthy periods of unemployment, were stigmatised as unemployable; the constant stream of salesmen at the door, begging for a standing order for a newspaper in return for which the householder was offered a gift — I obtained my first electric iron by agreeing to take a certain newspaper for a period.

Is it a wonder that some of the inheritors of this past feel that they are paupers in the Welfare State? That there are those who prefer to suffer deprivation rather than claim legitimate benefits? Sociologist Peter Townsend quotes people's responses when interviewed on this subject: [21]

'. . . I've never liked to cadge. I don't go running for help!'

'I don't want to tell people all my affairs. They ask too many questions. I'm proud, I suppose.'

'I'm a bad one for pleading . . . They wouldn't allow me anything. I'm awful about asking for anything. I'd rather starve than ask for a penny.'

'I don't like the idea of going to ask for it. Your pension now . . . you have a right to that . . . The Supplementary Benefit is not like something you're entitled to.'

'The pension is different. Everyone has a right to that. But the other, they have to come round every six months or so asking questions.'

I was asked in a radio interview why pensioners accept these humiliating conditions; why do they not speak up for themselves?

To answer this it is necessary to look at the heterogeneity and the composition of the retired elderly, their conditioning in an atmosphere greatly different from that of the post-Second World War period and after. Pensioners are not a homogeneous group. They vary greatly in their expectations, their life styles, their financial position, just as do other contemporary age groups. Since women have a longer life expectancy, widows predominate. The conditioning of women of my generation would provide enough ammunition for Women's Lib to last them a lifetime! Remember that women did not gain the vote until after the First World War. Even then the husband generally decided on the political alignment: politics, economics — these were a man's domain. Resignation, submissiveness, acceptance, a dread of being accused of 'moaning' — these were womanly virtues. In some households, the man was referred to as 'the master'. It was a waste of time to educate girls.

Working women had a hard life: their time was generally fully occupied in the endless fight against economic insufficiency — budgeting for a family on a shoestring. Expectations were low, they became accustomed to a life of comparative deprivation, just as an animal in a cage becomes accustomed to the limitations of that cage. Labour-saving appliances were not for them. This social aspect, the polluted atmosphere of towns and cities, the stress caused by insecurity, the neglect of incipient ill-health — all these take their toll in old age.

And why was this suffering swallowed and accepted in silence? My generation were conditioned by a culture in which obedience and uncomplaining fortitude were unquestioned virtues; where social injustice and an inequitable society were regarded as natural laws:

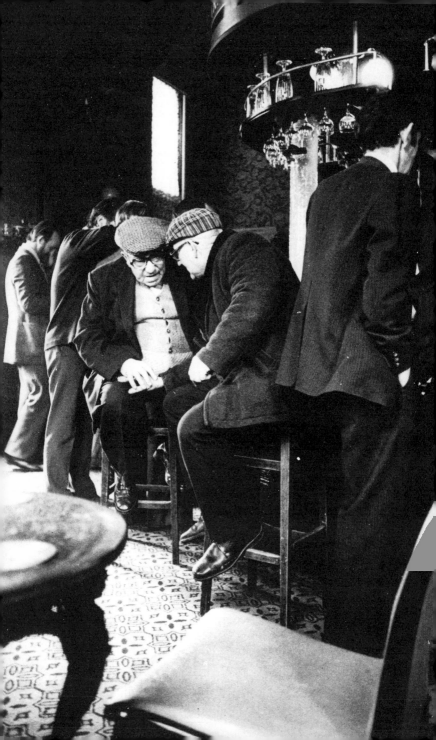

'Human nature has always been the same. It will never alter.' You were disciplined to accept your position in life, the *status quo* going unquestioned. But social conditions determine consciousness. Living now in an age of scepticism, weighed down by outmoded ideologies and traditions, it is difficult to realise that this is still 'our time'. Jeremy Seabrook writes of the working class elderly:

They have lived to see their customs and rituals fall into desuetude, their accredited beliefs spent, their received ideas suddenly used up . . . and when they handed on to their children the only life they knew, enshrined in the family treasures now abandoned, the children laughed and refused them and went their ways.[22]

Soon, nearly a third of a century will have passed since the Second World War; over sixty years since the First World War began. To the present generation, these wars must seem as remote as the Wars of the Roses. Students of the first war now believe it was fought because of the inability of statesmen to stop its escalation; whereas for many of the survivors, now in their eighties, it was a great and glorious crusade, despite the hideous conditions of trench warfare and the disillusionment after the holocaust. In many cases, the only reward for these survivors has been the conviction that they risked their lives for their country. If this belief is denigrated or debunked, they are diminished. Time was when to show that one had served in the war was to expect respect; in some cases it might help in achieving employment. This did not last long, of course, but still wartime experiences were something to reminisce about. However, glory fades; it is hollow at its best. Although the world is still racked with wars, the danger of another world war, which could be a nuclear one, makes it imperative that war should on no account be equated with glory.

I am reminded of a novel by Richard Aldington[23]

which ends with an epilogue in the form of a poem.
Eleven years after the fall of Troy, about forty of the
old warriors sit in the sunshine, showing their wounds,
talking about the war and their sufferings, the grey
hairs thick on their heads. A young boy says to his girl:

'Oh come away; why do you stand there?
Listening open-mouthed to the talk of old men?
Haven't you heard enough of Troy and Achilles?
Why should they bore us forever with the old
    quarrels of dead men
We never knew, all dull forgotten battles?'

And I thought of the graves by desolate Troy
And the long agony and how useless it was.
And I, too, walked away
In an agony of hopeless grief and pity.

Another difficulty experienced by many is the inability
to accept the tremendous changes in monetary values,
exacerbated by decimalisation, and in working-
conditions and expectations. After all, Royce of Rolls
Royce used to pay his apprentices 5s. for a 100-hour-
week. Conditions and wages for servants before the
First World War were abominable. Thus, 'I never in my
life *had* £20 a week,' a pensioner will declare, unaware
that this is well below the pay of the poorest paid
worker today. Such a remark shows that the speaker
has not grasped the actual fall in monetary value and the
changed living standards. At the same time pensioners
feel they are being fleeced because they are perfectly
well aware that a 20p loaf is costing them the equivalent
of the old 4s.!
    Of course it is not only the working classes that have
suffered the traumatic experience of this overwhelming
acceleration of the rate of change. We elderly all have
to come to terms with the present, and it is just as
difficult for the well-off to rid themselves of the past.
My generation, in all classes of society, have seen the

very foundations of their morality and beliefs collapse. There is a terrible sadness in lost illusions for those of us who had visions. To search in the ashes for fresh dreams when the cold midnight wind blows over the desert of our years is as difficult as was the relinquishing of our illusions. We may have suspected there were no certainties — it is another thing to experience it. Here is the essence of a terrible alienation. We are as strangers from another planet. How much do sociologists and psychologists, who spend their time peering at us through their microscopes, measuring our reactions and performance as though we were Skinner's rats[24] — how much can they possibly understand our past in a world now so remote? Their academic training and life style totally unfit them for an understanding of the lives a greater portion of these elderly have led. Experience is the only reality.

Little wonder if so many of my generation save themselves from the vertiginous effects of change by becoming first anaesthetised, then segregated, finally alienated. Nevertheless, I believe this disengagement is in part a myth that has grown as a result of mis-interpretation. Many of us, despite the burden of our past, can and do adapt to a changing ethos. As Simone de Beauvoir points out, there are some old people who refuse to be defined as '. . . reduced, diminished individuals, struggling to remain . . . human beings'. To those who have to plead need and answer the searching questions of the Social Security officials, the diminish-ment is total indeed, for it includes the sacrifice of human dignity. The endeavour to preserve a minimum of dignity in the midst of such deprivation is truly nothing short of heroic. Many do miraculously retain a desire for dignity and independence. The past is not for such as these; they *demand* to be integrated into the present.

Youth has always been the time for rebellion — but in the past its voice has been quickly snuffed out, as much by economic pressures as by the ever-present voice of authority. Today the young are much more vocal. They question everything. To many of the old, this questioning is not only insane but intolerable: the old 'know' that certain basic principles are right — the importance of the family unit, patriotism, knowing one's place in society and accepting it unquestioningly. Thus the young completely disrupt their world, and there is no longer any solid ground under their feet. Many today feel strangers in a world which smacks of licence and corruption. Of course it is wrong for young people to accept blindly existing standards: every generation has to 'find out for itself', and the current young are going at it bull-headed.

But after a lifetime of fighting against economic insufficiency, conditioned to low expectations — probably one of the greatest barriers between the young and old today — it is almost impossible for the aged to re-examine terms of reference that have become integrated into their personalities. To question them, to examine them with fresh insight in the light of a changing world is appallingly difficult. For never forget that many of us feel that our social milieu *does not entitle us* to more than a minimal subsistence; that to accept flagrant injustices, a third-class life with sweet resignation in old age is a sign of maturity; that nothing can be done — things will always be the same. All too often, therefore, a rise in the subsistence level is regarded with deeply-felt gratitude.

So rigidly automatised has their thinking become, so immured in the past are they by educational and societal influences, wedded to a traditional morality which prevailed in the early part of the century, that many elderly regard the affluence of those at the top as God-given and accept the flagrant injustices, the chicanery and corruption that from time to time are revealed in the press, as a sort of sacrosanct and natural law.

To sum up: within our society there still exist rampant nationalism, racism, ageism. We are hierarchically, chronologically, intellectually and ideologically divided. Individuals are segregated into little groups completely insulated against any understanding of each other and lacking the desire to do so. In such a spiritually sick society, is it surprising that many people can only bear existence by hiding from this reality, by ignoring the dualism within themselves that our society has created?

And while we watch, with bleary, half-comprehending eyes, let us laugh at the macabre dance of financiers, manipulators, speculators and monetary commissions. Those vainly trying to keep a worn-out, long over-played game going, shuffling and reshuffling the cards haphazardly, altering the rules from time to time to try and keep our geriatric social system functioning. For it is not only the old who are senile, who suffer from rigidity of the mind, from decrepitude of the brain. Many statesmen all over the world are victims — whatever their age. They too have been conditioned and programmed by their societies, so that they emerge as anachronisms in a changing world.

Re-educating the Elderly

I believe passionately that a continuing system of education available to the elderly is one of the keys to contentment in old age, and I shall devote some space to describing my own experiences in this field. Perhaps it might encourage those teetering on the brink who are feeling, as I sometimes did, 'Oh, it would be nice, but why bother? I'll be dead before I qualify!' But as R.L.S. Stevenson remarked, 'to travel hopefully is a better thing than to arrive . . .' Of course it is necessary to have an objective; but I myself have discovered that very special rewards lie in this particular kind of journey.

Dr. Elizabeth Monkhouse, a member of the committee that drew up the Russell Report on Permanent Education, speaking on an Open University programme, said:

The European concept of further education envisages a society in which . . . the learning needs of all citizens would be catered for . . . in its basic planning, structure and expenditure. The traditional notion of a terminal age for education as somewhere between sixteen and twenty-five would be abandoned, and the curriculum of the younger ages reconsidered in the light of what is to come in adult life.

Attitudes towards 'education' will have to change radically: it will have to be envisaged as a long-term process. There must be day-release for all those who want it throughout their working lives. Short-term residential courses for those with more leisure — pensioners, for example — must be far more widely available. And society at large will have to be re-educated about the learning potential of the elderly. For I am not speaking in terms of 'it would be nice if . . .' Automation, earlier retirement, improved health

Working on the allotment

care, resulting in increased longevity will mean that a vast body of the 'new' elderly will *very soon* be in desperate need of further education, occupation and help of all different kinds.

'The myths about the capacity to learn being reduced by increasing age are very tenacious,' writes Sydney Jones in an article in The Technical Journal. 'Where growing incapacity *is expected* with increasing age, this expectation influences many people more powerfully than perhaps we recognise.' He quotes two psychologists at Queensland University in Australia, who offered instruction in German for retired men and women aged between 60 and 91, people 'representative of a wide socio-economic range including former waitresses, telephonists, teachers and civil servants'. Instruction material and methods were novel and appropriate to people of widely different experience. 'The results were quite startling. At the end of six months, with three

classes per week, 50% of the students had achieved or surpassed the standards expected of fourth year secondary school children.' Even more important, they found that

these scholars gained greatly in confidence. Many began to branch out into new fields of skill and knowledge acquisition. Their social life was enriched too, through regular, purposeful meetings with their peers.

Today, many elderly people are at last starting out, as I did, on the road towards further education, many being greatly helped either by evening classes or by the Open University. A man of 82, who has already graduated there, hopes to achieve a doctorate in philosophy; another woman there who is 72 has just graduated and she too intends to continue working towards an Honours Degree. The following letter was read out on the OU's programme, 'Open Forum', in 1975.

Let me say thank you for preserving my sanity which from time to time I am in fear of losing through sheer loneliness and isolation. I'm a 60-year-old office cleaner, rising at 4.40 in the morning and spending 30 to 60 minutes in study before starting the day's work . . . I go off to work thinking of how merchant control of government could affect the çharacter of fifteenth-century Florence. The day wears on and a busy office keeps me on the move. The working day ends, the set book which I hopefully took to work in the morning is brought home at night unopened. My good, hard-working husband tells me to get down to my books while he prepares our evening meal. I feel a bit of a fraud when . . . I'm going over the same lines time and time again, listening to all the noisy distractions which a working-class district emits . . . This is real loneliness and isolation . . . Then I think of my tutor's warning against intellectual isolation and develop a bad guilt complex!

Certainly my own experience has taught me something of the enrichment that can follow the plunge into further education. In spite of poor health, whilst still employed, I was able to accept my ailments philosophically because I was deeply involved in my work and stimulated by contact with fellow students and teachers. Although I was afraid of deafness, the deterioration was slow and I managed to forget my fears most of the time. But when I retired they all suddenly overwhelmed me — as did a new-found loneliness. I was seized with the suspicion that I had *always* been alone, that it had merely been muted by the presence of others and the sense of 'belonging'. It is a condition that has been voiced time and time again by the divorced; yet in old age it is more intimidating, partly because the family have gone, as has all hope — or indeed desire — for a new partner.

These experiences generally served to convince me of the harmful and dehumanising effect of retirement on many of the aging. If at the same time one also suffers the loss, as I did, of a life-long partner, it can be a truly traumatic experience. Now, wherever I went, however affectionate were family and friends, I was conscious, as never before, of being a visitor, anxious not to overstay my welcome. In short I felt something had to be done. Then, one day, I read about the Open University and at once saw I could perhaps recover my self-esteem by finding a way back to life and stimulation. Was I still educable? I certainly had experience and a life of wide reading behind me. Could I acquire some wisdom? Could I make my life meaningful? Well, it would be a challenge, a voyage of discovery — as demanding, in its way, as that voyage undertaken by Sir Francis Chichester.

But I was still unsure whether I would be able to study at the level demanded. I therefore decided to test myself by following one of the National Extension College Gateway courses. I did so, quite successfully, gaining an 'A' grading in the English exam, and four 'high' gradings and two 'average' in the psychology/sociology papers. This was promising, and more — exciting!

Not long after I was accepted by the Open University. At first I was exhilarated by the challenge that was offered. I felt sure that in spite of my age, and the length of time that had elapsed since I had attempted any serious study, I would be able to cope — and my tutors were most encouraging. However, I made a bad start. I could not hear, and had under-estimated the frustration I would experience through my inability to cope adequately with broadcasts or lectures because of this. Clarity rather than volume was the stumbling-block, and I hated having to admit my disability. The week at the Summer School completely shattered me. Not only could I not follow the lectures, I was unable to read notices above eye-level, and was as yet too ashamed and too age-conscious to let anyone know of my difficulty. The lecture halls were about a mile away from the halls of residence and a shuttle bus service was employed. I did not know that the lay-by from which the buses started had been altered, and I found myself waiting alone, panic-stricken, for a bus that never arrived. Having to walk, arrive late and enter a room in the middle of a lecture was for me an excruciatingly humiliating experience.

Then a Senior Counsellor from the university came to see me, and I told her of my difficulties over deafness. She suggested that I should consider joining the hard-of-hearing group at York University; she would make enquiries about financial help from the Students' Hardship Fund to assist with the tuition fees — and she would ask that my examinations be taken at home with an invigilator present.

I felt wonderful after that, and rushed ahead like a house afire. I gained the requisite credit in the Social Foundation course that year, and passed the Humanities the following year. Encouraging counsellors and tutors were a wonderful help. One of my counsellors seemed to sense when I was not 'with it' and took pains to integrate me into the group. I enjoyed the course immensely.

My experiences at York University were such as I shall never forget. I could never have carried on without the unfailing support of the teaching staff. All this, at my age! I was made to feel that I really belonged there. I was inspired and no longer feared deafness when I found myself with stone deaf students, and noted not only their fortitude, but the marvellous way in which they were able to handle their environment, to converse by lip-reading and remain keen, alive and happy. I should imagine we were one of the happiest groups there. Under the supervision of Dr. Vida Carver, Chairwoman of the co-ordinating committee for disabled students, and Gerald Hales, research psychologist, and their team, everything went smoothly. They had an electronic print-out machine, a sign language translator, and induction loops for those with hearing aids. Lecturers spoke slowly and through a microphone. It was an incredible experience. Apart from the light shed on course material, I came to terms, for the first time, with my failing senses, and decided it would not be the end, whatever happened, so long as I kept my mental and critical faculties alive. Now, a portable loop hearing aid has been devised by the RNID, specifically to help students like myself with perceptive hearing loss. I have also widened my circle of acquaintances and made some very valued friends in the process of discovering new interests.

Working with the Young

I believe that one aspect of education today has been sadly neglected: children have far less contact with the aged now than they once did and as a result can learn little at first hand from those walking history books of the recent past, grandma and grandpa. This is doubly sad, since I think it is only the young today who are prepared to ignore our current image and seek for themselves the people that stand behind the mask of old age. There is no doubt that young people are coming to terms with the world of the old. Even when they do not understand it, they accept our world — and are in the forefront of the protestors who take action on behalf of the elderly.

In view of this breakthrough, our educationalists must help the young further in gaining an understanding of their immediate roots, so that knowledge can aid their kindly instincts. In fact, an adequate understanding of the cycle of life is missing from the curriculum entirely.

Perhaps we can also learn lessons from abroad. *Age Concern* recorded (Spring, 1974) the very different attitudes that prevail today in China:

There is still a widespread acceptance that the elderly have much to contribute to the community . . . one role accorded to elderly people in the Fung Qua residential area was to help in the education of young children. The experience of an old person in China spans a period of momentous change in their society, and who better to teach contemporary history? Just as workers come into Chinese schools to teach industrial production, so old people come to talk about the old days.

Integration between the aged and their grandchildren provides a valuable education and pleasant contact for both, while shutting the old away in geriatric ghettos merely widens the gap. We may not be able to teach the

young how to adapt in a changing society, but we *can* teach them about their recent past and its values in a way that no books can.

In many ways the work of Task Force is representative of much that is being done by young people for the elderly. This organisation operates in the London boroughs and its activities include: 1) running Clearing Houses involving young people in community service, particularly relieving loneliness among the old; 2) working at the educative aspect of community service from the volunteers' point of view, termed 'social education'; 3) investigating the needs of old people and experimenting with new ways of meeting them. They realise that the image of the 'do-gooder' of the past has to be avoided. An important factor that makes Task Force unique is that all the staff and volunteers are young (the average age of its staff is 23). In this way, they are bridging the generation gap, as well as encouraging the growth of understanding among the young. As Task Force themselves note, the more sensational aspects of adolescence — violence, promiscuity and drug-taking — are news; youthful idealism is not. Among their staff, the working day extends well into the evening. Self-help has become an increasing part of their programme, and elderly people are being encouraged to play a more active part in the community and especially to speak up for themselves.

Task Force's efforts with young volunteers have resulted in the most astonishing and hopeful results. In 1974 the following was published in their journal:

It is not difficult to underestimate the limited horizon of some of the children who offer to become volunteers ... In one school in North Kensington, for example, not one volunteer had ever had any relationship with a person of their grandparents' generation. Those who befriended elderly people, through Task Force, visiting them regularly and being fed tea and reminiscences, were introduced to a world of which they had no cognizance, and developed a sympathy for the old which may only be derived from direct contact and identification. In Chelsea, one young boy from a broken home calls in twice a week to 'his' old lady, who has no family of her own. She adores him, and he has found stability and a purpose in life. This example is by no means exceptional.

The great education theorist, Ivan Illich, has been urging for a long time that education should not be restricted to any one specific age group. 'If there were no age-specific obligatory learning institutions,' he says, '*childhood* would go out of production.' The kind of 'de-schooled' society Illich pleads for would help break down the barriers between young and old. Genuine education comes from contact with people — including the elderly who have their experiences to share:

Young volunteer visiting an elderly woman

Elders can be consultants on which skill to learn, which method to use, what company to seek at a given moment. They can be guides to the right questions to be raised among peers and to the deficiency of the answers they arrive at.[25]

The methods used in most school 'social study' periods pale when compared to those used by Task Force — that is, if and when they manage to obtain permission to conduct education inside schools.

Task Force staff and a teacher try to breathe life into the third year Social Studies course at a Catholic Comprehensive. There were five periods a week during the summer term. Ninety kids (more used to the geography of everywhere but Paddington, the history of politicians even more remote than Harold and Ted, the algebra of boredom, monotony, the literature of the great dead men) find themselves being asked to consider the mathematics of why the old lady across the street cannot afford to eat properly, the chemistry of young people's relationships, the poetry of human existence in Paddington now.[26]

The five periods were divided into two weekly sessions every alternate week. Time limited the scope of the course to the consideration of two underprivileged groups — the old and the young. 'What's it like to be old?' If only some of the scions of the privileged classes could have the same opportunity of learning about reality! But theirs is another form of alienation; they will never know what life has been like for the majority of older citizens.

Chapter 5
Health and the aged

Look to your health; and if you have it, praise God, and
value it next to a good conscience; for health is the
second blessing that we mortals are capable of; a
blessing that money cannot buy.
Izaak Walton (1593—1683) *The Compleat Angler*

The greatest medical experiment of all time was
unleashed on a hopeful but wary British public in 1946
— the National Health Service Act. Its Report, the
product of many committees, working together over
several years under the guidance of Sir William
Beveridge, was ambitious, idealistic and thorough. It is
thirty years since the Act, embodied in the Report,
became law. How many of its fine intentions have
become reality? Among its objectives, these important
aims were clearly stated:

To divorce the care of health from the question of
personal means or other factors irrelevant to it, and
encourage the obtaining of early advice and the
promotion of good health rather than only the treat-
ment of ill-health.

Another, equally worthy, intention was to 'ensure that
everyone, irrespective of means, age, sex or occupation,
should have an equal opportunity to benefit from the
best and most up-to-date medical services available.'
Yet to what extent have the aged achieved either of
these 'equal opportunities'? A government minister
has admitted that many of Britain's hospitals are still
archaic museums. Author Gerda Cohen[27] asks:

How did matters stand when the National Health
Service put all hospitals on an equal footing? Almost
without exception the working-class chronic sick
inhabited (ex-) Poor Law Infirmaries, some being

Geriatric ward

administered by Public Health rather than Public Assistance, but few changed in anything but their title.

It is my contention that it is impossible to separate the problem of old people in hospital from the wider one of their situation in society generally. For many of the disabilities and illnesses suffered by the elderly can be attributed, as we have seen, to the hardships they have suffered throughout life. By the time old age is reached, it is all too often impossible to mitigate the results of deprivation, pollution and stress. Pre-retirement courses may come too late to remedy the harm already done. The manner in which we still treat our aged reflects, only too accurately, the way we think and feel about them. As Gerda Cohen observes, in spite of the various government departments which enmesh the aged, their final years are so often deprived of either dignity or love. She describes, for example, conditions in an old people's home she visited:

Men and women were kept apart, even to segregated benches in the cavernous dining hall. 'One couldn't mix them,' the matron said with a touch of distaste. 'Their habits have gone astray' . . . 'Our facilities are grossly inadequate,' stated the doctor, 'just smell the lavatories,' throwing one open and startling the occupant, whose piteous eyes filled with rheum. 'Sorry grandma,' he said . . . no toilet paper was in evidence. 'They ask for it as needed . . . anyway, they're used to torn-up newspaper.' Marching back to his room, past old women huddled by the heating pipes, he gave a short laugh: 'Thank God, I can afford to maintain my mother in a private nursing home!'

Gerda Cohen makes striking comparisons between our treatment of the elderly and that available in Sweden. She writes of one scheme outside Stockholm, where a modest commune has built their frail old folk a block of flats with a hospital on one floor. She describes the two-room flats for couples, while single pensioners have bed-sitters. The beds have to meet Swedish orthopaedic requirements, she states, and residents are allowed to bring their own furniture with them if they wish to do so. They have the choice of either cooking their own meals, or having them provided in a communal dining-room. *Twenty-five nurses cared for seventy-five patients.* The sick bay was generally empty, despite the advanced age and frailty of some of the inhabitants.

Dr. Alex Comfort has written that the scope of geriatric rehabilitation should in fact be very wide indeed, since a surprisingly large proportion of elderly people are disabled solely by lack of such things as well-fitting teeth, spectacles and suitable accommodation. He refers scathingly to the medical superstition that nothing can be usefully done for the old, who must learn to live with the consequences of human mortality. Of the so-called necessary ills of old age, Dr. Comfort writes:

Many of these are not, perhaps, so necessary as we have assumed, but really spring from the effect of society's attitude towards them. *We may make old people socially old by retiring them,* we may even by the same token make them physically old, *for mind, body and society integrate in a person to a degree that can still amaze us.*

Dr. Comfort suggests the setting up of special clinics where the elderly may have periodic health check-ups. Not only would the establishment of such clinics and the education of people in their use be economic in the long run, they would also provide statistics for research into gerontology, along the lines of Manchester's Geigy Research Centre. He also suggests there should be greater co-ordination between medical clinicians and biologists. Obviously, the emphasis should be on improving the fitness of the retired, in view of the growing number of people who are living into old age: the high cost of hospital treatment of infirmities thereby being reduced.

Another, equally invidious cause of neglect has recently been revealed: research shows that many qualified doctors are avoiding work that brings them into contact with old people. Gerontology, as a branch of medicine, has come to be regarded as the Cinderella of the profession. A report entitled 'Attitudes Towards Geriatrics'[28] demonstrates that lack of trained medical staff is today a fundamental problem. While 13% of the population was over 64 years of age in 1971, they were yet occupying 33% of general medical beds in England and Wales — while the numbers of qualified staff have *decreased.* The report continues:

It is unlikely that the number of consultant physicians in geriatric medicine will increase to meet service and training requirements for the future, especially when the elderly increase to an expected 7.3 million in 1981 . . .

Interestingly and hearteningly, however, this study shows that young medical students have a far greater human interest in older patients than the qualified junior hospital staff, who think more of career prospects. Thus, '. . . without a change in the system, the present number of consultant posts will only be maintained if overseas graduates are persuaded to accept these appointments'. The report continues,

We must educate CMS (Clinical Medical Students) about geriatric medicine, the reality of today, and, more importantly, the potential of tomorrow. Our results show that these particular students are certainly willing to learn.

An article in the *Lancet*,[29] underlined this same problem: 'Most medical graduates shun posts in geriatric medicine as part of their hospital training.' Candidates for senior positions, says the writer, are here faced with little competition: 'This poor recruitment into a mainstream of practical medicine exists in a decade which will see another million added to the elderly population and a 20% increase in the over-75's . . . yet most junior staff had a career-oriented bias against geriatric appointments.' In a recent letter in the *Guardian* a geriatrician wrote:

As a geriatric specialist, I find myself frequently repeating a short prayer: 'From Welfare Homes and Geriatric longstay wards may the good Lord, my family, my friends, and enlightened medical profession and a caring community kindly protect me.'

A recent and encouraging innovation has been the establishment of the Geigy Research Unit on Geriatrics at University Hospital, Manchester, under Professor Brocklehurst — I believe the first of its kind in the country. As the Professor says:

The medical problems of old age should command high priority in resource expenditure if a society wishes not only to provide for its older members as each of us would be provided for, but also if it is to avoid the economic burden of a vast mass of disabled and dependent old people.

He passionately believes in putting into practice what he preaches. Apart from excellent research undertaken there, the building itself is pleasant and the equipment and day-care rooms are bright and comfortable. The wards are attractive, the patients well-dressed and the atmosphere cheerful. Above all, the staff firmly put into practice a policy which is geared towards rehabilitation, and point the way in which care of the aged must proceed in future. Here, enlightened doctors and nurses are trying to fan the winds of change into a tornado that will sweep away this blot on our so-called civilisation. But this is just one hospital among

thousands. Cut-backs in health and welfare services and, above all, insufficient recognition of the magnitude of the problem, will in no way help to encourage other hospitals to pursue the same 'pathfinder' course.

I was shocked at Gerda Cohen's description of the enforced segregation of the sexes. Surely the social stimulation which the other sex provides would be more likely to promote interest in appearance and combat apathy? After all, elderly men and women are allowed to congregate together in clubs. Any advance that might prove offensive to another patient would soon be stopped just as it is outside institutions — but at least it would make life more exciting. And why should it be distasteful? Simply because they are old? Why not ensure that elderly women have every opportunity to make themselves attractive, have their hair styled, their faces made up if they so desire, facial hair removed. This can be important remedial treatment. It is tragic to see old people lying apathetically in bed, their eyes unfocussed, unseeing, or sitting about listlessly. I recently visited a home in one of England's wealthiest towns where I was shaken by the sight of elderly women sitting on chairs placed around an empty ballroom. The door was kept locked and there they sat, doing absolutely nothing.

A stroke, a fall, broken bones, general ill health or any condition which renders an old person unfit to live alone may well land any one of us in such a home. That fine psychologist and author, Barbara Robb, wrote in *Sans Everything*[30] of 'the unwary elderly carted off into geriatric ghettos under the impression that they are being taken for a drive in the country'. Condemning the practice of spending 'most of the money on younger patients and very little on geriatric patients who have worked hard all their lives,' she continues:

We cannot dodge the accusation that we, as an advanced and civilised country . . . are treating a very great

*number of our old people, who in their time gave us
what we have, in a manner that is far worse than merely
barbarous.*

Does Kafka's beetle image remain in the minds of those
who have yet to find themselves so transformed — at
the mercy of a society that can only regard them as
objects for the dustbin, swept out of sight as quickly as
possible? As with the German people during Hitler's
regime, the defence mechanism of disbelief operates —
a defence that lulls the mind up to and beyond the
point where sensible preparations and precautions can
be made and taken . . .

I have had heart-breaking letters from many of
Barbara Robb's 'unwary elderly': one from a man who
was in an extreme state of distress. When his wife went
into hospital neither of them was told that she would
be put into a geriatric ward. He found her bewildered,
frightened, without dentures or spectacles, so shocked
that she lost her powers of speech. He and his family
were horrified and applied for permission to remove
her at once. Back home, and without medical help, he
nursed her back to seeming normality. But the shock
had been too much for her — she had a heart attack and
died. He approached various authorities, bewildered
and angry at his loss, but all they would admit was that
she had 'deteriorated' *after coming out of hospital.*

Health for some
So what of the Health Act's 'equality of opportunity'?
I will quote only one or two examples. Today there is a
growing tendency for large firms to pay subscriptions
to medical societies so that their senior executives and
managers can have periodic 'check-ups', as well as
various paying advantages. In this way, firms also gain
regular reports on the health of such employees, as
well as being able to obtain tax concessions on their
payments. A woman reporter recently described her
experience of just such a screening at a London medical

centre at a cost of £45 for men and £50 for women.

A list of the directorships of some of the private Provident Societies makes interesting reading. For instance, directors include a consulting surgeon of four hospitals; a specialist at the Charing Cross, Queen Charlotte's and Mount Vernon hospitals; a former director of the International Investment group; and a former Conservative Minister. In view of this formidable line-up, one can but admire the courage of the Labour Party, backed by hospital workers, in their attempt to cleanse society of this iniquity. Unfortunately, there are consultants who are prepared to use devious means to justify actions which they hope will obstruct any effort to build up in this country a medical service which will benefit rich and poor, the privileged and the unprivileged alike.

This is obvious from such schemes as the Private Patients' Plan which is outlined in a circular signed by Lord Brook of Wimbledon, an eminent thoracic surgeon. It was aimed at providing specialist service for a prosperous minority, giving unlimited cover for hospital charges and specialist fees up to £7,500 per annum.

In spite of my ability to live in the present, as I climb from the seventies towards the eighties I am a haunted woman. Who can foretell what may befall us, physically or mentally? My own — luckily premature — experience of what it feels like to find oneself apparently on the verge of senescence and incontinence may serve as a reminder to those whose 'defence mechanism' still runs on well-oiled wheels.

My health has never been very good, but I have been used to this for some years now. Six years ago I was studying hard, travelling and enjoying my family — that year I was spending Christmas with my daughter. Flu had gone the rounds and one morning I awoke to find myself as transformed as Gregor Samsa had been. I had the most appalling depression, accompanied by feelings of nausea, and a bitter, dry mouth. It was decided I had gastric flu — it was going the rounds at the time. But it was quite unlike any flu I had experienced before. The symptoms lasted a fortnight; one night I fell asleep and awoke to find myself back to normal.

Shortly after, my son-in-law died suddenly. I had been devoted to him and felt poignantly my daughter's grief, as well as my own. I was aware of a sense of shame that I should still be alive while my son-in-law, so young and so much needed, should have died. I even wondered whether, unconsciously, my daughter felt this too and resented me. Still, after a while, I carried on successfully with my Open University studies.

One evening in the following May I went to bed quite happily, looking forward to a visit to my other daughter. The next day I awoke with the exact repetition of the same violent depression, again accompanied by violent nausea, a bitter taste in the mouth — and a paralysing feeling of lethargy. Because of the suddenness and persistence of the depression I saw my doctor. X-rays, medication and examination revealed nothing physically wrong. At the end of an appalling five weeks the symptoms again vanished as suddenly as they had come.

I took stock. Retirement, a declining bank-balance and an increase in the *tinnitus* (the medical name for unceasing noises in the head) I had suffered for some while, eye irritation, rheumatism and hearing-loss must be taking their toll. Yet, apart from the *tinnitus,* I had more or less adjusted to these various complaints. (Only other sufferers know what it is like to be afflicted with this 'noises in the head' disease. Sometimes, after learning to tolerate the incessant cacophony, a new and sudden internal sound can again make life quite intolerable.) Were these all contributory factors to my new and nameless disease?

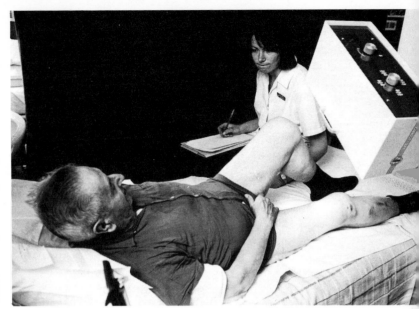

The following September it attacked again. I was staying with my sister in Swanage and enjoying myself immensely. We had had an enjoyable day at Poole and I sank into sleep with the sigh of satisfaction that goes with pleasant tiredness after a happy and lively day. When I awoke, the burden of intense melancholia once again possessed me. This time it did not go away. I will not repeat the symptoms — the same, only worse. Finally my doctor advised me to see a neurologist and I agreed. In fact, he made an appointment with a consultant psychologist. The day I saw her I was in the deepest despair, all hope gone, full of loathing and self-hatred, quite unable to talk, think or act. And yet, such was her personality, so bright and cheerful was she, that I suddenly found myself involved in a lively discussion about Tennessee Williams and the actor, Richard Burton! She asked me if I would be prepared to go into Delph Hospital for a short stay. I agreed, only

101

realising later that this was part of the famous Winwick hospital, a mental institution. I suddenly became fatalistic, resigning myself to the inevitable, in much the same way, I imagine, as certain people face approaching death. 'This,' I told myself, 'is the onset of senescence.'

The hospital was badly in need of decorating and refurnishing, the decor resembling nothing so much as that of a public lavatory without the fittings. The ward was cold — a large room with only one fire. The food was terrible. One memorable meal was a portion of flitch of bacon which was uneatable, accompanied by black pudding with the label still on! Another was of whitish stew which reminded me of the joke about the Frenchman who, when presented with a plate of porridge by a Scotsman, asked whether 'it was *to be* eaten or *had* been eaten . . .'

In spite of the extreme kindness of the nursing staff, I was treated to an appalling battery of pills. My circulation deteriorated and I was always cold. A friend brought me a hot-water-bottle; but for some inexplicable reason I was not allowed to use it — perhaps they thought I might try to commit suicide by swallowing the stopper! I awoke one morning to find myself covered in diarrhoea. This, I decided, was the end. Not only was I now psychotic — I was also incontinent. I would commit suicide. I saved sleeping tablets, planned to ask for home leave, and with the aid of aspirin and alcohol would finish it all off. But it wasn't so easy. 'Bring me all the tablets you have in your locker!' commanded the staff nurse one day. I asked, 'I suppose you'll never let me out of here now?' To my amazement she replied, 'You could go today — we could not prevent it!' A ray of hope — and another one later when it was discovered that one of the many tablets I'd been taking had caused the diarrhoea. If only they had told me at the time of this possibility, how much suffering I would have been saved!

When I finally left Delph, it was arranged that I should see a psychiatrist at the local hospital once a month. I agreed, for my experiences had left me full of doubts. I went to the appointment with some temerity, determined, in my own mind, that if I were subjected to any of that nonsense such as 'Who is the Prime Minister?' I would immediately reply, 'Stanley Baldwin!' All in all, I was beginning, though very slowly, and not too confidently, to regain something of my old spirit.

In fact, the psychiatrist was a charming, friendly man who talked to me freely and easily, and I found myself enjoying a general conversation with him, feeling I was being neither manipulated nor patronised. I mentioned that I had taken up the Open University course again, and he heartily approved. On my next visit I showed him some of my work, and he pronounced it incredible, especially considering the sedation I was having. He remarked, 'You must be stretching yourself to the limit in the circumstances.' I asked if this was unwise. He said it was the best thing I could do, and modified the medication to help me. Soon, of my own accord, I dropped sleeping tablets, anti-depressants and most of the tranquillisers; though I kept some in reserve in case I became agitated, and took one at night to help me ignore the increased head noises.

When my psychiatrist left to take up another post, he wrote to me saying 'Do not be afraid of senescence, nor of becoming a geriatric problem. There are no signs of that.' So now I keep the letter handy and when I want reassurance I re-read that sentence. I was much moved, for he knew my examination was pending, and in his letter apologised for not informing me that he was handing me over to another psychiatrist. He had not mentioned it because he knew I had the Open University examination hanging over me. I was very touched by his thoughtfulness. His letter finished: 'May I say that I consider it a privilege to have met and conversed with you.' I felt humbled that he should so express himself, for it helped to give me back my self-esteem. I had gained much confidence from having met him and this enabled me to go on from where I had left off. Now, whenever I feel discouraged or depressed, I re-read that letter too.

I was then transferred to the woman consultant I had met on my first visit, who was so charming that it was a tonic to converse with her; I greatly missed those chats when they ceased, for she certainly continued what my psychiatrist had begun. I had in the past regarded the word 'psychiatrist' with a wary eye. In fact, had not the word 'neurologist' been employed in the first place, I would probably have opted out of the appointment. One day the consultant said suddenly, 'Why don't you write a book?' When she repeated it on another occasion, I, just as suddenly, said, 'I will!' I had thought a lot since I had been in Delph, and inside me was growing a smouldering anger at what I suppose I had always known, but now felt, passionately, and had an urge to express.

An article by Sir Ferguson Anderson stresses the importance of preventive and remedial action:

. . . the spirit and service given by old people should make it essential that they be given good attention and first rate hospitals. Indeed, no health service can carry out other essential obligations to the whole community unless the elderly are adequately cared for.

He emphasises the necessity for a positive policy of seeking out illness and points out that the traditional self-reporting of diseases is no longer reliable, stating:

A methodology has now evolved, beginning with the ascertainment of or seeking out illness in the old person's home, and one way of doing this is by asking the health visitor to visit every individual in the community of 70 years of age and over. [31]

Alas, in practice, the after-care of elderly patients leaves a great deal to be desired. I meet and hear of people who have been sent home to cold rooms, or to poverty, while unreasonable delays occur in follow-up treatment. There is insufficient rapport between hospitals and family doctors — and, above all, there is a severe shortage of health visitors. I myself, living alone, have never *seen* a health visitor, even after coming out of hospital following a cancer operation. Many elderly people fail to report incipient signs of what might become serious health deterioration because they fear the all-too-common accusation of hypochondria.

A vast amount still needs to be done about the diet of patients in after-care. Hospital food seldom caters for the special needs of the aged, and thus, at a time when the patient needs building up, the diet is inadequate or inappropriate. Though Meals on Wheels supply an absolutely essential service, dietary needs get lost in the savage demands of our inflationary economy. Protein, for instance, is absolutely necessary to maintain vigour in old age (it will be noticed that those elderly who can afford a sufficient quantity of meat, fish and cheese are not seen shuffling along, wrinkled, bent and twisted). A study by Griffiths and Brocklehurst revealed that 41% of old people admitted to hospital were deficient in Vitamin C and 50% in Vitamin B.

But even when after-care — and indeed the care of the aged generally — is of a high calibre, I feel that there is a great danger of treating patients as children, thus encouraging them to accept this regressive role. Instead of being kept immobile, whether within hospital or without, skilled treatment, physiotherapy and the supervision of qualified geriatricians would ensure that a number of those previously confined to bed or a wheel-chair should be able to live a more normal life.

The importance of mobility and rehabilitation is stressed by all geriatricians. Dr. Ivor Felstein, a geriatrician and writer, has described[32] the new

Hairdressing at day hospital

Geriatric day hospital

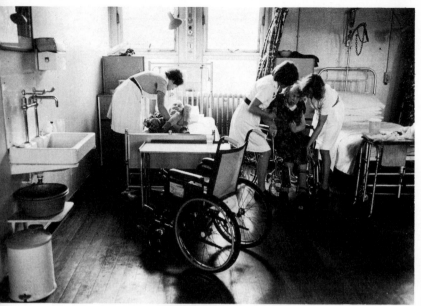

approach to this problem: instead of passively accepting
that the patient's condition is 'inevitable', attempts are
now being made to discover root causes in each
individual case. He cites examples of confused minds
and points out a variety of possible causes which have
been totally ignored until very recently: a full bladder,
temporary loss of fluid, anaemia, vitamin deficiency,
lung congestion or badly monitored drugs, such as
sedatives and tranquilisers. In fact, he has discovered
that there may be several causes over a period of time,
each one demanding more than one type of treatment.
The resultant improvement in health and spirit totally
justifies this kind of treatment, without considering
the money saved by avoiding the expensive care of
the 'immobile' patient. Dr. Felstein cites a case where
a confused old woman, after *three* lengthy examinations,
was found to be suffering from anaemia. When this was
rectified her mind cleared and she was able to return to

normal life.

Dr. Bernard Isaacs' report in *Age Concern* on old people in the east of Glasgow is significant in this context:

The illnesses of extreme old age were dominated by four symptoms: immobility, instability, incontinence and intellectual defeat . . . By studying a sample of old people who died after attaining the age of 65, we were able to demonstrate that two-thirds of the aged population experienced one or more of these four symptoms of dependency in the period which preceded their death and while they were living at home; one-third were incontinent, almost as many became abnormal, and two-thirds lost mobility.

Hypothermia

A report made by the Centre for Environmental Studies states that an average of 60,000 more people die in the six cold months of the year than in the warmer months. They add that hypothermia is one of the main causes of death in the winter months. In Denmark, where all rooms are required to be centrally heated, it was found that no cases of hypothermia had been recorded. Since no such laws exist in England — most houses, in fact, not being centrally heated at all — it is hard to see how old people can afford to keep alive during a bad winter.

I myself have a council flat. Last winter my wall thermometer showed an average temperature of around 57°F. After I received an enormous electricity bill I enquired whether the Social Security Department could help me. They asked if I was already on Supplementary Benefit. I told them I was not, to which they replied: 'Then you are not entitled to any aid whatsoever. There is therefore no point in an officer calling upon you.'

Hypothermia is an extremely complex condition by which, until very recently, the medical profession was baffled. A vicious killer, it is now proved to be particularly dangerous for the neglected and underprivileged elderly. A report, part of a larger survey on old age sponsored by *Age Concern,* has been written by Dr. Ronald Fox, entitled 'Warmth and the Elderly'. I have quoted extensively from it in the following pages by kind permission of *Age Concern,* the journal of the National Old People's Welfare Council. The author has drawn his material from many sources.

Dr. Fox points out that the evidence that elderly people live in grossly inadequately heated accommodation is overwhelming. Medical reports confirm that this is the single most important cause of hypothermia — death through loss of body heat. He quotes from such a report, published in January 1973, based on a study of the homes of 1,000 old people:

Clearly many of the rooms were much too cold for comfort. In 754 cases the temperatures were at or below 65°F, the minimum level recommended by the Parker Morris report on council housing; the proportion is even greater if the 70°F recommended for old people by a recent Department of Health and Social Security leaflet is applied. In 537 cases the temperatures were at or below 60.8°F, the minimum temperature specified in the 1963 Offices, Shops and Railway Premises Act. A number of subjects were living in exceedingly cold conditions. In 106 cases, morning living-room temperatures were at or below 53.6°F.

The study continued: *So far the only single factor to have any . . . value that has emerged is the receipt of supplementary benefits . . . which offers a crude means of identifying poorer old people . . . The cost of fuel is undoubtedly a major worry for old people; 375 of our respondents replied 'Yes' to the question 'Would you generally like to have more heat in the house?' and 91% of them gave 'too expensive' as a reason. There is a disturbingly large number of individuals with low body temperatures who are already receiving supplementary benefits. The Supplementary Benefits*

Commission considers that the basic benefit scale rates cover 'all normal needs' including fuel. The Commission also has discretionary power to award a weekly addition for extra heating in certain circumstances. In our national survey only 3% of pensioners in receipt of supplements said that they were receiving a fuel allowance. In answer to the question 'Do you know that in certain circumstances old people can get extra money for heating?' 74% replied 'No'. Obviously the availability of extra heating allowances . . . needs greater publicity. The Health and Social Security leaflet 'Provision for Heating' is helpful in this respect but is not sufficient by itself.

Another source of evidence comes from a survey of heating needs of old people in Islington, carried out by volunteers of the Islington Task Force between January and April 1971 and entitled 'Old and Cold in Islington . . . a question of survival'. In its conclusions it states

'This report has demonstrated that large numbers of old people in Islington suffer extreme discomfort each winter as a result of cold weather. Previous work on hypothermia has shown the danger to health which this entails and several tragic deaths in the borough last year gave more evidence of the seriousness of the problem . . .'

This survey closes with the words: 'The Islington Borough Council has the power to act in many ways to improve the lot of our old people. Nothing less than a strenuous effort both to give immediate help and to bring pressure to bear for long-term change is likely to achieve the improvements which are necessary.'
The same Task Force group reviewed the situation a year later and wrote a report entitled 'Left in the Cold: Final Evidence of the Suffering of Pensioners in Cold Weather'. The following are quotes from this paper:

*Out of 931 old people living in eight London Boroughs,
230 said that they were too cold during the day to live
comfortably and 190 that they were too cold to sleep
comfortably at night . . . It is clear from this that . . .
damp and draughty housing presents heating problems
for many old people interviewed and is a highly
significant factor in the causes of the inadequate
heating revealed by the survey . . . The findings support
the view that the widespread poverty among old people
is the most important cause of inadequate heating, for
this determines not only expenditure on fuel, but also
on food, clothes and housing, all of which affect the
individual's ability to keep warm . . . Only about 46
of the 617 people in receipt of a supplementary
pension had heard of the heating allowance . . .*

A significant percentage of ordinary retirement
pensioners (13.7%), experienced severe discomfort from

inability to meet their needs for warmth . . . Yet there is no provision in the basic pension for exceptional needs, not even for those who just fail to qualify for supplementary pension.

Yet, *in 1961*, a government survey[33] stated:

'We think it is time to recognise that a home without good heating is a home built to the standards of a bygone age. The nation has enough of those already . . . We propose that the minimum standard should be an installation capable of heating the kitchen and the areas used for circulation to $55^{o}F$ and the living areas to $65^{o}F$ when the outside temperature is $30^{o}F$.'

Euthanasia

Of course, one of the greatest dangers that will face us within the next decade when (should the prognosticators be proved right), there will be a 20% increase in the number of over-75's, is that the medical and allied machinery will break down. When so many elderly will be demanding the treatments that will in theory be available, then it seems probable that the shadow of euthanasia will loom ever closer in a society unable to cope with its members . . . I would like to outline my thoughts here, as I feel I am voicing the fears of many elderly people.

The senior consultant at St. Chad's, a hospital for terminal care, has said: '. . . medicine is about getting people better. And most of those who come here don't get better.' Yet he is totally against euthanasia — though, he says, 'I wouldn't resuscitate a 90-year-old with a serious stroke.' He goes on to say that the elderly are reachable. 'Even the senile and demented, living twenty or thirty years in their emotions, will still respond to kindness.' Legalised euthanasia is merely an escape from the responsibilities of caring for the sick and infirm. It is not only unethical but dangerous — dangerous because we can never be sure that 'the final decision' necessarily involved will be taken by the highest level of caring, compassionate and disinterested groups of people. Surely others besides myself felt their blood run cold when, on a television programme, *Saints Alive* (25 October 1975), we heard the views of a doctor representing the Association for Legalised Euthanasia. How brusquely he brushed aside the speakers who were pleading for more care for the elderly sick — with the remark that 'the economy couldn't stand it'! He offered instead what he called voluntary legalised euthanasia. With all the sedatives that are today handed out to the sick elderly to keep them quiet, it would take little pressure to get a large number to sign such a document. I don't believe the medical profession has a monopoly on incorruptibility — they are people like the rest of us, who find it easy to justify actions when they suit the purpose. Furthermore, diagnoses can be wrong: witness the number of people wrongly incarcerated in psychiatric institutions through lack of understanding and knowledge.

Gitta Sereny, in her striking book, *Into That Darkness,* describes how at the beginning of the last war in Germany, slowly and insidiously, Hitler's 'Euthanasia Programme' first came to be accepted by ordinary, dedicated people working in hospitals. Their scruples were eventually over-ridden by the mounting horrors (at first only known to very few people) of the extermination camps. German hospitals and nursing homes like Schloss Hartheim and Hadamar, even if not set up for such a purpose, were, she says, training grounds for the future administrators of the death camps. Franz Stangl, for instance, worked at Hartheim, 'keeping the records', before being made Kommandant of the Treblinka extermination camp in Poland. The famous pursuer of Nazi war criminals, Simon Wiesenthal, declares that Hartheim was one of several 'schools for murder'. It was, he says, organised like a medical school, 'except that the "students" were not taught to save human life but to destroy it "as efficiently as possible".' Experience shows that acceptance of the practice of euthanasia could very easily become the first step on the road to mass euthanasia, as it did in Germany — first for the sick and the handicapped, but ultimately for the aged as well.

To sum up: in the medical field I am fighting for:
1   More geriatric training for all doctors and specialists
2   More merit payments to be allocated to this side of the NHS
3   Better liaison between the health and social services, and between them and the family doctor
4   Improved living arrangements which will include proper after-care, heating and special equipment such as the installation of telephones for the crippled or bed-ridden.

Finally, if hearts are not stirred by my pleas, let me appeal to the heads of all those who still do not appear to have grasped the inescapable fact that *it is uneconomical* to wait until the human machine breaks down and then to fill much needed hospital beds with the ailing, the sick and the dying. True care of the aged means, in effect, care of the *aging.* Thus, life-long health care for each and every individual must become our unalienable right.

The photographs in this chapter (except the one on page 112) were taken at St. Pancras Hospital: either in the wards, often the best place for patients who need constant care and attention; or in the day hospital, which offers treatment for patients living at home. The day hospital assesses patients' practical skills and gives training and help in the use of aids.

Chapter 6
What is to be done?

Nothing, not God, is greater than one's own self, one's difference, one's uniqueness.
Walt Whitman

I have tried to point out some of the social attitudes which must change before the elderly can enjoy the dignity and sense of worth which is the right of all human beings, in all phases of their lives. But meanwhile a number of steps will have to be taken to ensure the well-being of our deprived elderly *now*. Immediate action should be pursued in some, if not all, of the following areas to improve their living conditions. I list them because they may serve as guidelines for newly-formed Action Committees or Worker/OAP Associations.

Housing
In the August 1975 issue of *Age and Aging*, a pilot survey revealed that 24% of houses visited inhabited by the elderly were not suitable as living accommodation for people aged 75 years and over. It is the job of housing committees to see that *no* elderly people are allocated accommodation in high-rise blocks. All rooms, flats and houses occupied by the aged must be centrally heated. Where existing houses are inadequate, wardens must be appointed to check such matters as heating and lighting. Free telephones must be installed in all types of accommodation where pensioners over 75 live alone, or where pensioners of any age are crippled. Installation of free 'phones 'more than doubled the chances of being alive, and trebled the chances of being both alive and in their own homes,' wrote Peter Gregory in a study on the subject. He estimates that the cost, based on a 1970 pioneer scheme in Hull was: 'an initial outlay of £3,000,000 . . . annual

running costs £1,250,000' — minute sums in terms of human happiness — and the GNP!

Health

The minimum requirement is regular health check-ups that would, if properly organised, soon become automatic for both patient and doctor. A lot of old people haunt the G.P.'s surgery just *because* they feel neglected. Give them the proper care and attention and you would see a great falling-off of hypochondriac visits. District nurses and health visitors could be used much more relevantly in this field than they are at present, which would relieve the initial burden on GP's themselves.

Psychogeriatric care must be vastly improved. One practical step towards the realisation of this goal would be the immediate upgrading in pay and status of doctors in this least popular branch of medicine. A pensioner's representative should sit on all committees handling such patients.

Far greater attention must be paid, during the training of *all* doctors, to the ills and ailments of old age. More too must be paid to the diet of the aged, and help given where necessary.

Pensions

For all fully paid-up workers, we should aim at a minimum of two-thirds of the average wage, linked to the cost of living. No more disguised Means Tests. Instead, those whose incomes are thereby brought into a higher bracket would be automatically taxed.

All limitations on earnings after retirement must cease; they already do after the age of 70 (for men) — so why not at 65? By working all their lives, people ought to qualify automatically for their pensions. Whether they decide to work or not after qualifying seems to me to be nobody's business but their own. Professional men frequently do work on for many years

after the official retirement age. Why must 'workers' be penalised?

Travel

Ask anybody nearing the age of retirement what they most want to do and the chances are, eyes alight, they will answer, 'Travel!' Yet how many of them are actually able to afford to do this — however much they may have saved with that end in mind? Fares generally must be reduced for OAP's, perhaps by the issue of cheap tickets on production of a pension book. Without for the moment considering the deserved pleasures of travel, much loneliness could be avoided if old people could travel to visit their scattered families and old friends. Air and shipping lines should also cater for those aged whose relatives live abroad.

An article entitled 'Mobility and the Elderly',[34] studied the particular problems of domestic travel.

For the most part, transport planning is dictated by the travel requirements of the working population . . . yet these may well be unsuited, indeed unrelated, to elderly needs.

Movement in urban areas even for the fit is becoming increasingly difficult. The loss of such local facilities as the corner shop, local butcher and the post office, together with the dispersal of many old established communities, all too often has resulted in an increase in the distances between homes and services, while no new solutions have been introduced. Walking — often a slow and laborious process for an elderly person — now involves the added danger and discomfort of heavily congested roads, fast-moving one-way traffic systems and light-controlled crossings which require quick movements and good eyesight.

Improving the Image

The best place to start polishing up our image may well be the media: with their vast audiences, they are the creators and purveyors of many harmful stereotypes. Much ground has been covered in recent years in the fight against racial discrimination. If pressure can be brought to abolish slogans and advertising containing implicit racial prejudice, so we can also be vigilant for signs of prejudice against old age — never far below the surface. The cosmetic industry, as I have already said, has much to answer for with its never-ending yelps after eternal youth (is-your-skin-aging-type slogans), while some comedy series and dramas on TV are nearly as bad. Think about the comedy dramas you've seen over the years: how often have the elderly — excepting the rich or distinguished — been painted in a favourable light? Realistic and sympathetic elderly characters are seldom viewed on the television screen.

The Open University is in the process of setting up a course called 'The Aging Population', which takes the view that it is not only the old who should be concerned with the aging process — and here, much work on improving our image can be done. After taking such a course, the middle-aged would be in a far better position to prepare for their own old age — and could also give valuable help and practical advice to their less fortunate or less intelligent elders. For instance, they could learn about ways to help the aged in their own communities; they could start groups for still-active pensioners who want to do local part-time work. Many pensioners have written to me suggesting they could help other less fortunate pensioners than themselves, undertaking repairs in their homes, maybe, or use in other ways the tools of their life-long trades. Those with clerical skills could undertake typing, or help in sorting out their money affairs. A quite moderate organising talent is all that is needed to get these and similar projects off the ground. Once under way I am certain that they would bring unexpected rewards in the way of new friendships and companions.

However, I want to make it clear that while I believe that all the above objectives are important, they only answer short-term needs. They do not spring out of a natural response to the problems of the aged, but will have to be promulgated 'from above', as it were. It is only when developments in two vital directions receive universal encouragement that a proper existence for the elderly will become an every-day concern — namely, re-education which I have discussed in an earlier chapter (see p77) and political power.

We elderly have power if we only cared to exercise it, for numerically we are strong. Mr. David Hobman, Director of Age Concern, has this to say about our potential power:

. . . There are already enough retirement pensioners to vote a government in or out and to influence social policies on which their personal fulfillment depends. They don't have to accept the crumbs which fall from the rich (working) man's table. This fact has not escaped eight million American retired people who have already created a powerful political lobby, as well as an effective self-help organisation. It was also the pensioners' vote late in the day which influenced the election of France's President.

It will be different in the future, because the next generation of pensioners were not born in the shadow of the Poor Law. They will be better educated, as well as more articulate and politically sophisticated. They will understand how the system operates and know how to manipulate it as well as the professionals . . . We shall no longer tolerate the provision of services for others which we should not be ready to accept for ourselves . . . Now it is the turn of the retired . . . Pensioners of the world, unite![35]

In other countries, too, pensioners are waking up to their position. Action groups in Australia have as their theme song: 'Onward, old age pensioners,/Onward as to war' — the revolt of the elderly!

Even if industry and the nation are enriched in the Britain of tomorrow, even if the current economic crisis is overcome, the workers will always have to fight to participate in the country's economic growth.

The only way old people can keep pace with rising prices is by aligning themselves with the workers, who in turn can only benefit if they align themselves with pensioners and espouse their cause. For, of course, the workers' future status will be built on what today's pensioners can achieve. Otherwise, organised workers will eventually find themselves in the same position as today's pensioners. Unless they fight *now* they too will have no bargaining power when they retire. The trade unionists know that they have to fight step by step to safeguard their immediate future. When their services are no longer required what mercy can they possibly expect? The time to take action is whilst they have power. Those whose services are still vital to the economy can safeguard their own future, as well as help the present pensioner, by raising the matter of retirement pensions and by supporting the claims of pensioners, by writing to the press, and by letting their MP's know where they stand on this issue.

In fact, the TUC's statements on their attitude and involvement with OAP Associations is interesting. Their policy on pensions, broadly speaking, is parity of retirement age — 60 for both men and women; and an old age pension of not less than 50% of the national average wage. This would, if achieved, raise pensions for married couples considerably. However, while it is true that they passed a resolution at the 1974 Congress that labour would be withdrawn if pensions were not raised (which they were) they also insist that they 'speak for the *present* members of the work force' only

— i.e. its 11,000,000 working members. But *once people retire they automatically cease to be union members,* and thus cannot possibly exert pressure through their branches. Until this short-sighted policy is reversed we shall never achieve our objectives.

Little is done at national level. For instance, one of the largest Unions, the Transport and General Workers, admitted that retired members cannot vote, cannot be on committees, or stand for election! The only sop they throw in the direction of OAP's is the occasional support of the British Trade Union Pensioners Action Groups — by going to rallies and asking all workers to volunteer *a penny a week* to the Groups' funds. And even this activity is organised on a local basis only.

Thus pensioners who are already members of OAP Federations must build up powerful pressure groups to activate any and every government, of whatever complexion. All the elderly, whether ex-members of a union or not (and a large number of pensioners have never been unionised), will have to join forces before widespread change can be brought about. The TUC must, meanwhile, make itself responsible for all pensioners — especially for those who have spent their lives in non-unionised, low-paid employment and who now need desperately an umbrella organisation on a national level to build up an effective pressure group.

My own experiences in setting up an OAP Association in Lancashire might help others who are uncertain how to go about it. Mine — the Halton Workers' and Pensioners' Association — was formed in July, 1973. We were lent enough money to pay for the use of a community centre, and we then called a meeting of pensioners. A member from the Merseyside Workers' and Pensioners' Association was invited to speak. He suggested we form an association such as his; this was readily agreed to, and we then formed a committee which included two trade union officials, a district councillor, a minister of the Church of

England and a social worker. We had great support from building-site workers and received a large donation from one of the unions, with which we were able to repay our original debts. By 1974 there were over 200 enrolled members. Good coverage was secured in the local press and a rally was held at Widnes. Members also attended rallies in Blackpool, Manchester and London. Our association is currently moving ahead fast and membership grows.

It says much for the resilience of the human spirit that people like the militant and indomitable men and women I have met in Pensioners' and Workers' Joint Associations have a lot of fight left in them. From some of the letters I have already quoted, it can be seen that for many there is no disengagement, no meek acceptance. I hope the ex-Trade Union official who wrote to me has been able to use his past experience to good purpose. He said:

Since my retirement, on reaching sixty-five, I have felt most uncomfortable and frustrated at not being able to agitate for better conditions for pensioners, and have long seen the need for some positive and militant pensioners' organisation . . . I am convinced that there must be a number of pensioners who, like ourselves, are quite articulate; and if they could be contacted and organised we could conduct a most effective campaign for the improvement of pensioners' conditions.

He is now a member of the Merseyside Workers' and Pensioners' Association.

And at last pensioners *are* waking up. That other great organisation, the Old Age Pensioners' Associations Federation, never ceases to watch events and to fight injustices; they have put up a gallant fight for pensioners over the years. They have stated unequivocally that they stand for:

. . . the principle that old age and infirmity shall no

longer be subjected to utter despair . . . (we are) engaged in an unequal battle to get something better out of life than a meagre existence . . . we stand to strip old age of any pretence to pauperism, to ensure that henceforth they shall have not just enough to make life tolerable, but a sufficiency such as shall at least be in keeping with Christian civilisation . . .

The points from The Pensioners' Charter give me new heart. Reproduced in full as an Appendix, it may help as a guide for those who want to start their own militant group (see page 137).

I believe that the two greatest achievements of our country are the NHS, with all its faults, and the Open University with its many opportunities. I have learnt more during the past few years than in many previous years, and thus my life has been enriched. As I near the end of this book — a lot of which has, I know, been sombre — I think it is time I gave thanks to and for some of our champions: Jack Jones and Jack Dash; our Action Committees and National Federations; Task Force, Help the Aged and Age Concern — all of whom are wonderfully committed to our aid. The scientists too, who are campaigning on our behalf — people like Dr. Alex Comfort, Professor Brocklehurst and Dr. Ivor Felstein. I realise that vast changes must occur before their fine work can be complemented and widened. But if enough people can hold on to their dream, this too will surely become a reality. Because of them, the next generation of the elderly will inherit a different and better climate. I like to think that they will take up the fight when I am gone so that I can say, with that good, grey poet Walt Whitman, that

> *. . . I am glad,*
> *That you are here,*
> *That the powerful play goes on*
> *And you may contribute a line.*

Chapter 7

Gladys Elder — her life by Christine Bernard

The first and last thing about Gladys Elder is that she was a fighter. In the face of unbelievable difficulties — deafness, acute poverty and, eventually, a terminal illness, Gladys battled on throughout her life, the burning spirit of the reformer shining through to the end. It is not necessary to search far to find the roots of Gladys' zeal. Both her parents were deeply involved in the early Scottish Socialist Movement. When they acquired a 'revolutionary' label their children were ostracised by teachers and pupils alike. One of Gladys' early schoolroom memories is of a teacher praying for her socialist soul in front of the class. For this was the time, in a deeply conservative society, when rebellion against established institutions and morality was itself a sign of emancipation.

Gladys Mary Dunn was born in Glasgow in 1899, the eldest of four children. The family lived a more or less vagabond existence. For a while, the father was a travelling salesman. Her mother, a restless human dynamo, could never bear to stay in one house for more than a couple of years. She remembers her parents with love, for they were both lively, eccentric and attractive individuals. Because of her parents' political involvement — and because of their innate hospitality — people of many nationalities passed through the house — talking, making music, discussing and arguing vehemently. The great pioneer Socialist Jimmy Maxton and the anarchist Guy Aldred were frequent visitors; other friends were the Blatchfords, the charismatic Victor Grayson (who later disappeared under mysterious circumstances); not to mention the delightful Tom Groom, a cycling expert, who drove the Clarion Van round the villages preaching Socialism and, to announce his coming, stuck posters on the sides of cows. There was also the exotic Madame Sorgue, a socialist friend of her mother,

described as 'the most dangerous woman in Europe' —
as well as a constant flow of Russian refugees.

The Dunn house was full of books; and throughout
her life, books were an essential life support for Gladys.
Mrs. Dunn taught all her children to read at an early
age, and by seven Gladys was reading *Ivanhoe* to her
younger brothers and sister. Earlier in this book she
vividly describes the horrors of the only Edwardian
education that was then available for the poor; her
education was undoubtedly received at home. It seems
to have stood her in good stead; for when Gladys
began her own formal education some forty years
later, all the attributes of scholarship were present.

Another aspect of Gladys' character is shown in her
description of herself as an obstinate, rebellious child
with a violent temper when frustrated. She has recalled
the mixture of joy and horror when, in a rage, she
pulled the table cloth from the table — fully laid and
bearing the Sunday dinner!

Illness — the seventh and ever-present member of that
underprivileged family — early put in an appearance.
Through nursing a neighbour's dying baby in a slum,
Gladys' mother caught diptheria and was extremely ill;
later her younger daughter was infected and became an
invalid for some years. After a short but enchanting
and memorable period in the Yorkshire countryside,
Gladys left school before her fourteenth birthday, took
a secretarial course — and joined the underpaid British
labour force before she was fifteen.

When war was declared the family moved from
Yorkshire to Dundee so that her father, being unfit for
military service, could find work. For a time he had a
job. Then his activities in the No-Conscription Fellow-
ship were discovered and he was given the option:
give them up or loose your job. He chose the latter
and a pall of dark poverty settled on the family. They
moved from Dundee back to Glasgow, then trailed
from Glasgow to Liverpool and on to Manchester,

Gladys aged 15

living in a succession of cramped furnished lodgings —
the home having been dispersed.

Gladys meanwhile had taken a good job in London
at the Seaman's Union, and it was the money she sent
home at this period that kept the Dunn family alive. In
spite of a long working day she found time to join the
Suffragettes and worked with Sylvia Pankhurst in the
evenings — here again Gladys was in contact with some
of the liveliest minds of the day. But her father was
now almost permanently out of work and Gladys
decided she could help more if she lived at home.
Manchester, centre of the cotton trade, was now in the
grip of the great cotton slump and neither father nor
daughter could find work. Sometimes the family went
without food all day. Eventually the parents were taken
in by kind friends while the children (all four were
now growing up) cramped themselves into a cheap
room in a boarding house. At meal times they had to
resort to banging knives and forks on empty plates so
that the landlady wouldn't know that they had neither
food nor money until the end of the week — money
because Gladys had at last found another job.

When she was thirty, Gladys married an old family
friend, Frank Elder, a life-long socialist and idealist,
who had a small paper-bag business. His offices,
however, were more likely to be used as a socialist
rallying point, or as a shelter for the needy rather than
for financial transactions — and the business did not
prosper. By the time their first child was about two,
Frank was threatened with bankruptcy and Gladys
went out to work, though all that was then available
to married mothers were ill-paid temporary jobs. But
the Elders struggled on, snatching happiness where they
could, wringing some pleasure out of their hard lives.
Pregnant again at thirty-eight, and with the war clouds
gathering (both Frank and Gladys were both deeply
involved in the politics of the Spanish war, and lost

several friends who went out to fight there), illness struck once again. A sudden succession of severe illnesses attacked Gladys, both before and after the baby's birth, when she nearly died of pneumonia. But Frank was still in deep financial trouble and soon after the new baby's first birthday Gladys took a permanent job, paying someone to look after her. Wartime paper restrictions more or less put an end to Frank's business; the resulting worry and strain contributed to a long and painful illness from which he never really recovered. Fifteen years older than Gladys, he struggled on manfully only for a few years longer.

Gladys finally got a good job as a secretary as her children grew up. By 1949 she was attending evening classes — at last taking the first step towards fulfilling her life-long ambition to be a teacher. At the age of fifty, in the face of unbelievable odds (the least being a full-time job!) Gladys, with a broken hand, took the six-hour exam for her teaching diploma — and passed. Now, three evenings a week she taught for the County Educational Service, and attended other evening classes for further exams as well. In spite of chronic ill-health, within a year or two her full-time teaching career was under way. She was offered a lectureship at the Runcorn College of Further Education and she accepted it (on a lower salary) at the age of fifty-eight. Her delight at this achievement was one of the chief solaces of her later life — along with the joy she found with her daughters and grandchildren. At Runcorn, Gladys enjoyed the excitement of organising a full-time department from scratch, and the pleasure of being surrounded by young people.

When Gladys retired at the age of sixty-eight she found life pleasant enough for a while; she visited her family and travelled abroad, discovering much of Europe for the first time in her life. Then, as she movingly relates in a preceding chapter, a severe and long-lasting depression seized her. As she slowly recovered, the spirit of the reformer once again moved in her. She was now seized with the desire to do something about the appalling conditions under which so many of the old and the underprivileged existed. She sought out publicity and became quite a figure in the north of England, being interviewed by the press frequently, speaking on the radio and appearing on a David Frost TV programme. This book is the outcome of Gladys' unceasing efforts on behalf of the elderly; her pioneer work in organising militant groups of pensioners — meeting, and facing squarely, some of the root causes of the alienation of the old that shames our society. Her warmth, her quick tongue and her humour remained with her to the end: never one to take bureaucratic bullying lying down, in the last year of her life she rounded on a housing official and told him: 'Bureaucracy is cold: the icecaps are warm compared with you!' Before death swept her away, Gladys had all but achieved her final ambitions: the book was written — and she had acquired four of the six credits needed for her B.A. at the Open University.

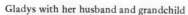
Gladys with her husband and grandchild

Postscript

Gladys died on September 27th, 1976. Only a few months before, in pain, deaf and dying, she was still able to write the following concise letter which was published in the *Observer* on April 18, 1976; and a poem which sums up her belief.

Pensioner's plight

As I read Mr Healey's explanation of the gain trade unionists would achieve by accepting his Budget without demur, illustrating how they will actually have *greater* net spending money, I shuddered when I reflected what the £2 increase in November would mean to me and others like me.

I have a teacher's small pension, which was, *unfortunately,* increased on 1 December by £1.60 per week. This meant 99p tax, and a drop in rent rebates of 40p a week plus a drop in rate rebate: a total *drop* in net income of 31p weekly.

The £2 increase in November will bring my income up to a gross total of £1,202.04 annually, or £23.12 per week. I shall therefore have £1.32 weekly to pay in tax. From my past experience, I think I may safely assume that I shall lose more than 40p on rent rebate weekly, and quite a sum on rate rebate, so that my net income will be lower than it is at present.

I cannot afford increases.

Gladys M. Elder
Manchester.

I Come from a Country that does not exist

They call it the World,
This place from which I come.
Racism, Ageism, Nationalism,
And Mammon-Profit —
What are these ghosts?
Emanation of an evil past
Dead of corruption.

No 'Brave New World' this,
No insect hive,
But one earth land and peoples
of infinite variety,
Where Mind triumphant soars,
Now undivided.

Power-lust and exploitation
The Brontosaurus past
That once enslaved mankind,
The legendary past
of myths and history,
How came resurrection?

Whence rose this land?
Whence these peoples?
Phoenix-like from ashes
of sacrificial fires,
They wingéd rose
To greet the rising sun.

Gladys M. Elder.

PENSIONERS' CHARTER
Prepared by the British Pensioners' and Trade Unions
Action Committee (London region)

This is a Charter of minimum demands which we feel
will restore Pensioners to a position of equality in
British society. It is meant for adoption by Pensioners'
groups and others concerned in the pensioners' struggle.
We presume they will want to use it as a discussion
document and promote its implementation.

DEMANDS
1 The Pension
There should be a guaranteed adequate pension which
is a fixed proportion of the national average industrial
(male) earnings. This should be 50% for a single
pensioner and 75% for a married couple. Supplementary
pensions should be abolished.

2 Guaranteed Housing Standards and Services in the Home
We believe that, wherever possible, pensioners should be
able to live an independent life in their own homes.
This means two things should be ensured:
a. There should be priority given to maintenance of
pensioners' and maximum provision of sheltered
accommodation.
b. There should be maximum provision of services by
local authorities, hospitals, etc. to pensioners to allow
them to remain in their own homes.
   Paragraph a. above means that Public Health
Inspectors and local authorities must give priority to
ensuring that the homes of pensioners are fit to live in
healthily. In addition, local authorities must be made
to build enough accommodation of suitable type (as
decided by pensioners) to cater for pensioners' needs.

Paragraph b. above means that the services provided by local authorities, hospitals, voluntary bodies, etc., must be brought up to the standard demanded by pensioners. We believe that pensioners will stand the best chance of remaining in their own homes if they are provided with effective services of the following types:
Social services — home helps, meals-on-wheels, etc.
Health services — health visitors, hospitals, G.P.'s, bathing, home nursing, chiropody, etc.
Social visiting, odd jobs, and welfare rights advocacy.

3 Pensioners' Power and Decision Making
Pensioners know best what their needs are, and so it is self evident that their voice must be heard. We demand that there should be recognition of pensioners' groups where they exist and financial and other encouragement (from the authorities and Trade Unions) for them to prosper. Pensioners should be involved in all decision-making which affects them, from deciding on levels of provision of services to running day centres, homes, lunch clubs and pensioners' rights offices. Pensioners' groups should be represented on social services committees, community health councils, etc. In short, wherever pensioners' issues are raised there should be pensioners' representatives.

Premises should be made available for pensioners to run rights offices, clubs, action groups, etc.

4 Taxes and Concessions
Special concessions and tax systems for pensioners should be abolished as unnecessary after the above pension scheme has been introduced. Pensioners should be on a standard tax code and basic pensions should be disregarded.

5 Educational, work and leisure opportunities
It is evident that an adequate pension will immediately bring broadening of pensioners' horizons. However, we feel that there should be an accent of opportunities

throughout life. As a start, places should be made available for pensioners in secondary and further education. Other work and leisure facilities should be provided as demanded by pensioners.

6 Health

There should be immediate pressure on local authorities to fully implement the Chronically Sick and Disabled Act. The importance of preventative medicine and social care should be recognised and the difference between the inevitable and avoidable consequences of growing old should be stressed. Area Health Authority Centres should give improved services and hospital discharge should be tightened up.

7 Transport and Mobility

There should be immediate action by all the transport authorities to ensure that transport facilities meet the particular needs of the old and infirm. In addition, there should be action to guarantee access to buildings for those disabled or using a wheelchair. Aids and adaptations within the home should be guaranteed by full implementation of the Chronically Sick and Disabled Act.

Text notes

1   Simone de Beauvoir, *Old Age,* Weidenfeld and Nicolson 1972.

2   J.K. Galbraith, *The Affluent Society,* Penguin 1975.

3   Alex Comfort, *The Process of Ageing,* Weidenfeld and Nicolson, 1965.

4   Joan Gomez, *Dictionary of Symptoms,* Centaur Press, 1967.

5   Nesta Roberts, *Our Future Selves,* George Allen & Unwin, 1970.

6   Lou Cottin, article in the *Runcorn and Widness Weekly News,* Feb. 1971.

7   *Pensioners' Voice,* published by the Old Age Pensioners Associations, 91 Preston New Road, Blackburn.

8   E.W. Busse and E. Pfeiffer, *Behaviour and Adaptation in Later Life,* Little, Brown, & Co., 1969 Churchill Press, 1970. See also: *Popular Trends 3,* HMSO Government Statistics Service, Spring 1976.

9   Erwin Stengel, *Suicide and Attempted Suicide,* McGibbon and Kee, 1965.

10   Walter Greenwood, *Love on the Dole,* Jonathan Cape Ltd., 1933.

11   Jack Ashley, *Journey into Silence,* The Bodley Head, 1973.

12   *Pensioners' Voice,* op.cit.

13   W. Rae Ashby, *Design for a Brain,* Chapman and Hall, 1960.

14. Lou Cottin, op.cit.

15   Michael Harrington, *The Other America: Poverty in the United States,* Collier Macmillan, 1962.

16   Jack Shaw, *On Our Conscience: the Plight of the Elderly,* Penguin 1971.

17   Simone de Beauvoir, op.cit.

18   Phillip O'Connor, *Britain in the Sixties. Vagrancy: Ethos and Actuality,* Penguin, 1963.

19 *The Lancet,* Jan. 4, 1975.

20 *Age Concern,* 1974.

21 Peter Townsend, *The Family Life of Old People: an Inquiry in East London,* Penguin, 1963.

22 Jeremy Seabrook, *The Unprivileged,* Penguin.

23 Richard Aldington, *Death of a Hero,* Chatto and Windus.

24 B.F. Skinner — a famous Harvard 'Behaviourist' psychologist.

25 Ivan Illich, *Deschooling Society,* Penguin, 1976.

26 *Task Force Journal,* 1974.

27 Gerda Cohen, *What Is Wrong with Our Hospitals?* Penguin, 1970.

28 J. Gale and B. Livesy in *Age and Ageing,* British Geriatrics Society, 1974.

29 *Lancet,* April 13, 1974.

30 Barbara Robb, *Sans Everything: A Case to Answer,* Aid for the Elderly in Government Institutions, Thomas Nelson & Sons, 1967.

31 Sir F. Anderson, in *Modern Geriatrics,* April 1975.

32 Dr. Ivor Feldstein, *Later Life: Geriatrics Today and Tomorrow,* Penguin, 1969.

33 *Homes for Today and Tomorrow,* HMSO.

34 *Age Concern,* 1975.

35 *Modern Geriatrics,* July 1975.

Suggested reading

Age and vitality. Irene Gore. London: George Allen & Unwin for Age Concern, 1973.

Arrangements for old age. London: Consumers' Association, 1974.

The care of the aged. Dennis Hyams. London: Priory Press, 1972.

Care of the elderly in Britain. Central Office of Information. London: HMSO, 1974. (C.O.I. Reference Pamphlet 121.)

Easing the restrictions of ageing. London: Age Concern, 1972. (Seminar papers.)

Guide to the social services. London: Macdonald & Evans for the Family Welfare Association, annual.

Health for old age. London: Consumers' Association, 1970.

Housing in retirement. London: Bedford Square Press for NCCOP, 1973.

Manifesto on the place of the retired and elderly in modern society. London: Age Concern, 1975.

Old Age edited by Edward Jones, Michael Heyhoe, Beryl Jones, London: Routledge & Kegan Paul, 1972.

Some old people's organisations

The National Corporation for the Care of Old People, Nuffield Lodge, Regents Park, London NW1 4RS, is an independent offshoot of the Nuffield Foundation, established to stimulate better provision for the elderly and to promote clearer thinking on social policy issues. Its two main functions are grant aid to voluntary bodies (not to individuals) and research and development.

Age Concern England, Bernard Sunley House, 60 Pitcairn Road, Mitcham, Surrey CR4 3LL, is the national organisation linking over 1000 Age Concern (Old People's Welfare) organisations throughout the country, which provide services such as day centres, clubs and voluntary visiting. It provides training and information services for local groups, publishes a variety of booklets, and works at all levels to improve the status and rights of elderly people.

Help the Aged, 8–10 Denman Street, London W1A 2AP is a fund raising and campaigning organisation helping needy old people throughout the world by the provision of food, clothing, shelter and medical aid. In the U.K. it promotes day centres, and its education department stimulates activities in schools.

Task Force, Clifford House, Edith Villas, London W14 works in ten London Boroughs where it organises volunteers wishing to visit and give practical help to the lonely and housebound elderly. It supports active groups of pensioners wanting to organise their own services, and at a national level produces occasional research reports.

Contact *Age Concern England* (tel: 01-640 5432) for further organisations which help the elderly.